'TIL STRESS DO US PART

Also by Elizabeth Earnshaw

I Want This to Work

'TIL STRESS DO US PART

HOW TO HEAL THE #1 ISSUE IN OUR RELATIONSHIPS

ELIZABETH EARNSHAW, LMFT, CGT

sounds true
BOULDER, COLORADO

Sounds True
Boulder, CO

This book is not intended as a substitute for the medical recommendations
of physicians or other health-care providers. Rather, it is intended to offer
information to help the reader cooperate with physicians and health-care providers
in a mutual quest for optimal well-being. We advise readers to carefully review and
understand the ideas presented and to seek the advice of a qualified professional
before attempting to use them.

Published 2024
Book design by Meredith Jarrett

Printed in Canada

BK06930

Library of Congress Cataloging-in-Publication Data
Names: Earnshaw, Elizabeth Y., author.
Title: 'Til stress do us part : how to heal the #1 issue in our relationships / Eliza-
beth Earnshaw, LMFT
Description: Boulder, CO : Sounds True, 2024. | Includes bibliographical references.
Identifiers: LCCN 2023056223 (print) | LCCN 2023056224 (ebook) | ISBN
9781649632579 (hardback) | ISBN 9781649632586 (ebook)
Subjects: LCSH: Couples--Psychology. | Interpersonal relations--Psychological
aspects. | Intimacy (Psychology) | Stress (Psychology)
Classification: LCC HQ801 .E25 2024 (print) | LCC HQ801
(ebook) | DDC 158.2--dc23/eng/20240116
LC record available at https://lccn.loc.gov/2023056223
LC ebook record available at https://lccn.loc.gov/2023056224

FSC
www.fsc.org
MIX
Paper | Supporting
responsible forestry
FSC® C016245

To Andrew, it's us against the stress.

Contents

Introduction

When I first opened my therapy practice, I purchased a small, beat-up, two-seater couch from IKEA's as-is section. It was fifty dollars and all I could afford. A friend helped me carry it up to the fifteenth-floor of a city building, shove it into my tiny office, and cover it with a brown slipcover. Since then hundreds of couples have sat on that couch as they yell, cry, laugh, and share with each other.

In those early years, the couples therapy I offered was fairly generic. Two people sitting side by side would tell me what was going on and I would coach them on how to communicate their frustrations with each other. While these skills are certainly important, the couples I was working with would come back week after week, sometimes year after year, complaining that while things had gotten better in some ways, they were still arguing in the same manner when things got difficult.

I was doing everything I had been taught to do in school and yet I was missing one key component—recognizing the role stress plays on how couples can navigate everything from intimacy to communication to decision-making.

A few years into my work, I got married following a whirlwind romance. Andrew and I met, moved in together, and got married all within two years. Everything was great until we had our first baby. Suddenly, I felt like I didn't know my husband or myself. We went from being happy and connected to angry and withdrawn.

I knew what was going wrong. We were too critical and defensive and too wrapped up in everything—our baby, our jobs, our activities—except each other.

I would tell myself exactly how to avoid the next argument, repair the ruptures, and build our connection. *Stop rage texting*, I would remind myself. *Even though I'm tired, I am going to put my damn phone down and listen when he talks to me*, I'd commit.

And yet day after day and night after night, I would behave in ways I couldn't even identify. And so would he.

One night, after a particularly bad argument, I spent time researching exactly why I was so unhappy. I came upon an answer—something called mental load disparity.

The mental load is defined as the cognitive effort involved in managing life responsibilities and decision-making. This might include planning a trip, researching which dentist your family should go to, remembering birthdays, and delegating chores, a type of labor that often falls mostly to women. As I continued to research the mental load, I became more and more shocked that not only had I never heard of it as a woman but also as a couples therapist. I knew I was letting my clients down by not pointing out this heavy burden in the relationship.

For the first year following that argument, I attributed all of our unhappiness to the way the mental load was being distributed in our family. I went on an obsessive journey to better understand how it wasn't only impacting me, but also my relationships.

But then, things with the mental load improved. My husband got better at noticing the toilet paper was low and became the only person in charge of doctor's appointments. Yet as I became less and less burdened with managing our lives, we still faced fairly challenging arguments and points of disconnect.

I was frustrated. If the communication skills I was taught in school and the mental load research I had so strongly grasped onto weren't making as big of a change in my relationship as I had hoped . . . what would? Were we doomed?

Then the pandemic hit. Everything in our lives changed drastically without notice, and my husband and I were grasping at straws to maintain our jobs, show up as loving parents, and take care of each other.

I experienced a paradigm shift. I realized it didn't matter how much I knew about relationships because if I was stressed out and overwhelmed, the "skills" I had weren't going to improve my marriage. Similarly, teaching couples communication skills in therapy wouldn't help if underneath it all was stress and overwhelm. Having nice conversations solves nothing when you're drowning.

Our relationship was sinking in a Swiss-cheese canoe. There were many holes—one being the unfair distribution of tasks—caused by too much stress in our lives. Not only would we need to improve how we distributed tasks, we would need to consider how many tasks we took on and how we coped with our burdens.

As I met with couples during this time, I started to realize something: stress was the cause of so many of their issues. The way they argued and the way they let each other down was only the tip of the iceberg. When you looked beneath the surface, stress was fueling the behavior they detested.

In graduate school, we learned very little about how stress influences relationships. Sure, we spent some time learning how it impacts our bodies, and therefore our minds, but when it came to relationship work, we were mostly focused on "skill building." Our classes focused on teaching couples how to speak, listen, and compromise, but not how to identify the role stress played in their inability to do any of those things.

Every week, couples come into my office blaming their relationship issues for their stress, when in reality, their stress is often to blame for their relationship issues. Again and again, couples share that they are failing; there aren't enough hours in the day to lean in at work, practice attachment parenting, show up for their Peloton ride, and take the dog for a walk, let alone take time to connect with their partner.

Prior to the pandemic, divorce rates were down. People were working to keep their marriages together and relationships were thriving. Since the pandemic, I've witnessed an unraveling in my office; couples are struggling more than ever.

They are struggling with each other, yes, but when it comes down to it, it's because they are struggling with life.

We are living through global crisis after global crisis and this has created much of our relationship crises. People are unable to connect; they feel lonely, depressed, and unfulfilled in their relationships. The last several years have caused couples to face all kinds of external stressors including health anxiety, political turmoil, financial uncertainty, working from home, childcare strains, loss of community, isolation, and more.

According to the American Psychological Association's 2022 Stress in America Poll, Americans are more stressed than ever. In particular, families are suffering, with 70 percent of parents saying that they believe they are under extreme stress when it comes to the development of their children and fears for their children's futures. We also know that families are under great financial pressure. Inflation has caused gas prices to rise 58 percent, the cost of food is up 6 percent, and housing costs continually increase, all while workplaces fail to pay salaries that keep up with rising costs.

Over two million women left the workforce during the pandemic, meaning that many dual-earning households significantly reduced their income at a time when inflation and housing costs were getting out of control.

More people than ever are unhappy with their jobs. Whether you call it the Great Resignation or Quiet Quitting, it's clear that people are leaving their workplaces in droves, only to find themselves more uncertain about where to go next to find the financial stability they crave. And on top of collective grief, instability, and workplace stress, people continue to navigate common personal stressors like parenting, health, domestic duties, and managing daily life.

People are drowning, and at the same time they are being told they should be thriving. Despite all this increased stress, pressures have never been higher—to be the perfect employee, parent, and fully actualized self. This is all leading to a crisis of shame. "I'm not a good enough mother." "I'm not a good enough ally." "I'm not a good enough partner." "I'm just plain not good enough."

This stress-shame cycle is having a disastrous effect on our ability to connect. And yet, no one is talking about the source of our biggest relationship issue directly. Although most might think stress is merely just a blip on the trajectory toward relationship fallout, I'm here to tell you it's actually the cause and our reactions to it are the blips.

When we are stressed, we begin to lose access to important tools like affection, humor, and problem-solving, which can have disastrous effects on our relationships over time. Although the messages from books like the *Year of Yes* and *Lean In* are powerful, they can actually lead people to take on more and more in order to believe they are doing something "valuable" with their lives. Meanwhile, the most valuable part of life—our relationships—are being neglected.

I want to teach you how to create a life that includes a mix of "yeses" and "noes" by leveraging the science behind good stress and bad stress. I hope couples can understand how to better protect themselves and their relationships from distress so that it's no longer wreaking havoc on their connection.

This might sound daunting, but I promise, you can do something about it.

I've organized this book in a unique way. Not only will I use my own stressful life experiences (having a baby, living through a pandemic, navigating terminal cancer in a family member, and job changes), but we'll also be following the progress of specific couples (an amalgamation of the real-life stories clients have shared with me over the years) as I work with them to alleviate stress in their lives. It'll be as if you're sitting in on a therapy session as I walk you through a relatable account of how stress can fracture your relationship and what you can do to heal it. I'll end each chapter with Session Notes, recapping the lessons we learned and outlining exercises to put them into practice in real time.

Over the course of the book, I'll reassure you that it's likely you aren't bad parents, bad employees, or bad partners. Rather, you're being put under undue life pressures that make it nearly impossible to feel good about yourself in these arenas, which heightens conflict, resentment, and disconnect in our relationships. The book will identify gender issues (such as the mental load and roles), sky-high parenting expectations, and our society's boundary problems (like constant access and low compensation). I'll also discuss the unavoidable facts of life that cause us stress, like finances, illness, loss, aging, and an unpredictable world landscape.

You'll be able to identify the type of stress you're experiencing—from acute stress to chronic stress, distress, and even eustress (the positive type of stress we need in our lives)—in order to better understand your circumstances and why you feel the way you do. My goal is to offer you hope through science, which has taught us a lot about how to keep our brains and bodies safe from stress. The first step is identifying stressors and how they are impacting oneself and one's relationships.

I'll also help you start seeing the aha moments in the unexpected ways in which you're actually playing a role in your own stress. You might not even realize it, but the time and energy you put into finishing that project or not setting correct boundaries are all fanning the flames of the stress fire. Our high-stress society is impacting our emotional, sexual, intellectual, spiritual, and emotional intimacy, and I'm going to show you how to let go of all the pressures and expectations and do less in order to save what's most important . . . our relationships.

I'll share solutions to protect you and your relationships from stress. You'll learn how to self-soothe, recognize when your body's reactions are flooding you, and understand why boundaries are critical in protecting our relationships. I'll even share communication strategies you can use in real time to start advocating for yourself and navigating your differences.

Stress is inevitable, but it doesn't have to consume your life or your relationships. If you're feeling defeated and unsure what to do to save your relationship, this book will give you the tools to take action now.

CHAPTER 1

Lessen the Weight of
the Mental Load

You are crazy. Really, you are crazy.

I repeat this to myself as I sit on the floor looking at the room around me. Strewn about are socks, T-shirts, underwear, mismatched pillowcases . . . and a banana peel?

While usually these clothes would be on the floor because neither my husband nor I can be bothered to walk them to the laundry basket after taking them off, this time it's because I threw them there. And now here I am, exhausted, tearful, and giving myself a big dose of negative self-talk.

I. Am. Absolutely. Nuts.

At this point, I have been up for twenty-four hours, give or take thirty minutes of "sleep" here and there. I am a new mom, and my son never sleeps. He has a serious case of FOMO that even my mom—who raised three children—says she has never seen before. Set him down for a second and he wails.

A few nights before, I had been out with friends and was telling them about George's refusal to sleep. They were skeptical. "Liz, he has to sleep at some point. It's just not possible that he is never sleeping."

And yet, it was true. George never slept.

Our society's rampant pressure in regard to perfectionistic parenting—books, Instagram posts, and mommy message boards—has turned me into an anxious hover-mother, and I think it's rubbing off on my son.

As I sit on the floor in an old T-shirt, feeling exhausted and frenetic, I reflect on the night before. It was like every night I've had since becoming a new mom. I zombied around the house trying to soothe my screaming baby for hours on end. Moving from room to room, holding him, rocking him, and then placing him into one of the six sleeping apparatuses littered through my house. When the only sleep device that worked, the Rock 'n Play, would finally lull him to sleep, I would stay up to watch him because I was afraid he'd roll over and die. The Rock 'n Play has since been recalled—I guess my anxiety wasn't totally wrong.

Last night was a little different though. I hit my limit. After finally getting George to fall asleep, I tiptoed into the kitchen and saw (and smelled) pots and pans covered in dried sauce from our dinner. There were noodles on the counter and unwashed baby bottles. And was that dog pee on the floor? I wanted to scream. I didn't, of course, because screaming wouldn't be good for the baby, I thought. And then he woke up, again.

I walked upstairs and heard my husband snoring. I wanted to murder him. But that *definitely* wouldn't be good for the baby. As I walked past our bedroom, I whispered under my breath, "I hope you die in your sleep."

"Huh?" he said.

I kept rocking our baby. Walking back and forth in the hall. The "huh" enraged me even more. "So you're telling me you can hear me right now? You can hear us right now? And you are . . . *sleeping*?!"

I gently put our wailing baby down ("Your stress becomes the baby's stress!"). Then, I walked over to the laundry basket and picked it up over my head, as if I was a wrestler and it was my rival, and body slammed it across the hallway.

Then, like a maniac, I started picking items up and hurling them everywhere. "HUH!? Well 'huh' this, you asshole! I fucking can't do this anymore! How the fuck are you sleeping? WHY DO I DO EVERYTHING AROUND HERE?" I started sobbing. I was enraged.

My husband shot up and said, "What the hell is going on!? If you needed help, why didn't you just ask me?"

Andrew got out of bed and walked over to George's room. He picked him up, looked at me, and asked, "Where is his sleep sack?"

I looked at him, defeated. "Why would I know where the sleep sack is any more than you would?" My eyes lowered into a slit and my mouth grimaced. I knew if I continued to talk, I would say nothing good, so I inhaled deeply, turned around, and walked out of the room.

As I listened to Andrew trying to settle George, I sat on the floor of the guest room, staring at the ceiling. The house grew quiet, but my mind was loud.

I sat there until morning, in a hungover-esque haze of rage. The stress and anger dripping out of my body, leaving me feeling sore and weak.

Now, this morning I'm so activated that I don't really know what to do with myself. I pick up my phone and do what all well-adjusted couples therapists do after a big fight—I angrily type into the Google search bar: "How can I get my husband to stop being an asshole?" There are a lot of articles. As I scroll, I come across a comic strip called *You Should've Asked* by someone named "Emma Clit."

I read the comic and see relatable images of a woman trying to make it all work while her partner sits on the couch enjoying himself. I take a deep breath of relief. I'm not alone. And then, I come to it. The part of the comic where everything is going astray in the home, the woman becomes upset, and her husband says, "You should've asked! I would've helped!"

Sounds familiar, I think.

I put my phone on the floor beside me and curl my head into my lap. I cry in that balled-up position for a while. I am so tired of asking. I am so tired of it all.

Over the next few days, I spend time looking into what the comic showed me I was experiencing. There are words for it—mental load, emotional labor, invisible work. These terms describe a burden I am all too familiar with. It isn't just going through the motions of daily living; it is the fact that I have to do both the physical labor of taking care of home and family and the invisible work of knowing it even needs to be done.[1]

It isn't that I can't handle parenthood; I just can't handle it under these conditions. I am carrying an unfair portion of the physical and mental load in our family—and I am suffering deeply because of it.

Mental Load: the invisible, nontangible tasks involved in running a household.

As I continue to research the mental load, I become more and more shocked that not only have I never heard of it as a woman, but also as a couples therapist. This is clearly indicative of a bigger social issue: not even couples therapy training programs were guiding us to think about the ways that undue burden and stress play a role in whether or not we can connect with people. And in that moment, I feel emboldened to understand the concept better for myself and my clients.

It's the morning after Laundrygate and I'm getting ready to head to work. It is 7:00 am and my hair is still damp from a last-minute shower. George is sitting in his swing after being fed and dressed for the day. I look at the clock and think, *Huh, the sitter is late. Hopefully she will be here in a few minutes.* I run back to the kitchen to move breastmilk from the freezer to the fridge so she can feed him and recheck my bag to make sure my breast pump is there.

I'm all set, standing by our front door waiting for Maggie to arrive to take care of my little guy. It is twelve minutes until my train leaves and she still isn't here. My heart is racing, and my stomach is clenched. I am not going to have time to go over everything with her before having to dart out of the house.

This is so unlike her—I am a mix of worry for her safety and panic for myself. I can't miss this train or I'll be late for my first client of the day.

Usually, my in-laws come to help with George while I work, but today they can't come until later and I am so grateful that Maggie can come and help me. I've got a team of support that I know most people don't have.

As I watch the clock ticking, coming to the realization that I am going to miss my train, I perseverate on the inequity in our home. My husband woke up this morning, got dressed, ate breakfast, and drove himself to work, on time, without a worry in the world. He didn't juggle getting a baby ready for the day while getting himself ready—I did. He didn't secure coverage for his parents' "day off"—I did. He doesn't have to wait until Maggie arrives—I do. And now, I am writing an apologetic email to my first client of the day letting her know that I have to cancel our appointment.

I use my fingerprint to open my phone and go into the Gmail app to email her:

> Hi Claire, I'm so sorry but I've missed my train and won't be able to meet for our appointment this morning. I can reschedule you for later today at 2 pm or tomorrow at 3 pm. Because of the inconvenience, I won't charge you for our next appointment.

Send.

I sit on the bottom step, staring at the door until I hear a faint knock. It's Maggie. I let her in with a smile and give her a big hug "Thank you so much for coming!" I say. I don't want her to feel bad for being late—she is helping me after all—so I don't say a word about the time.

I quickly walk her through what she needs to know to take care of George and run out the door and into the chilly November morning with wet hair and my coat shoved under my arm.

The ride into the office is usually a welcome relief. I get to people watch or scroll my phone absentmindedly. I get to just *be* without having to take care of anything or anyone.

Today though, I am anxious . . . *I wish I could do something to get the train to speed up. I'm already such a letdown at work*, I think. *I'm not as sharp as I used to be. I forget to respond to emails. Lateness is becoming a thing.*

My thoughts are interrupted when I hear a tall man at the front of the train car yell, "Next stop, Suburban Station." I stand up, moving toward the doors so I can be first onto the platform. *If I go fast enough, I can still get there in time for my second client* I think. As the train pulls to a stop and the doors open, I hop off and run, in heels, toward the escalator and then up it.

As I am nearing the top, in what could only be explained as Murphy's Law, my heel gets stuck in a crevice, and I fly forward, piercing my knee on the sharp, jagged edge of the escalator step. It hurts so badly that I nearly shout. I can tell something is very wrong with my knee, but I have to get to work.

I keep running and don't stop until I step into the elevator of my office building. I open my phone to a text from Maggie. "Does George have any clean bottles?" I click out of the text and walk to my office. As I step into the waiting room, I look down to see my Club Monaco slacks soaked in some sort of red substance. *Is that . . . is that fucking blood?*

Just as I am coming to terms with the fact that I am bleeding and that my slacks have a four-inch rip, I hear a voice beside me.

"Liz, you're bleeding! Are you okay?"

I look up to see Shaun, my next client of the day, and his wife, Lina, waiting for me on the couch under the bright fluorescent lights.

"I'm okay, sorry I'm late . . . feel free to head on back to my office. I'll be right there."

Couple Profile

Lina (36/F) and Shaun (37/M) have been married for ten years. They live in the city with their three children. Lina is a stay-at-home mom and Shaun works as a hospice nurse. Lina and Shaun come to therapy to solve high-intensity arguments.

I walk into my office after cleaning up my knee and take a seat. It's bright today, the sun is bursting through the large windows, illuminating the room.

Lina and Shaun have already taken their jackets off and made themselves comfortable. Lina's hair is pulled back into a messy bun, dark circles around her eyes. An oversized shirt rests on her tiny frame and she holds a coffee mug up near her face.

"I really don't know what to do with him. I am enraged," Lina says as she glares across the room. Lina and Shaun have been married for ten years and are facing a lot of stress. Because of the high cost of childcare, they've decided that Lina should stay home with their young children while Shaun works. Shaun's job is demanding, and while the pay is okay, it never feels like enough.

While Lina agreed to this arrangement, now and then it comes up that she misses working as a receptionist at a pediatrician's office. "I had my own time. I got to jog after work. It was exhausting sometimes, but it was nice to get the break from home."

On this particular morning, Lina is angry. She's just found out that Shaun has agreed to take on more hours at work when they already feel poor on time at home.

"I am going to be stuck with all of the work with the kids and you never think about that! You are truly such a selfish jerk . . . never thinking about anyone." Her lip is curled into a sneer and her left eyebrow is raised. She looks at him without flinching.

Shaun barely lifts his head to look back at her. He's depressed and collapsed, and he doesn't know how to navigate her disgust of him.

On other days, I've found Lina's contempt difficult to navigate too. But today is different. I look at her criticisms, her sneers, and her arms akimbo in a new way. Lina isn't crazy or mean. Lina is pissed. And maybe it is for a good reason.

Maybe she is justified in her anger, I think as I try to ignore my throbbing knee. *Maybe, like me, she feels like she has to do it all, know it all.*

Don't project . . . don't project . . . don't project, I remind myself.

But I can't stop.

"Lina, I have a question for you. Do you feel like you've got to take on the job of remembering everything all the time? Of taking care of it all? Is that why you're so pissed?"

"Well, yes, that is absolutely it. I remember it all. I do it all. And if I am not doing it, I am delegating it. It doesn't matter how much Shaun helps me, it never will be enough because it's me who has to know about the helping. And when he helps, I need to carry that entire process too. And I never escape it. He gets to go to work, but I am always here dealing with our lives."

"This is so unfair," Shaun interjects. "You don't notice my contributions and I don't understand your problem—you are staying at home all day while I go and deal with the stress of work. You always make me the bad guy, but what is really happening here is your . . ."

Oh no. Here it goes again . . . Lina criticizes—using absolute terms and put-downs—and Shaun responds with defensiveness—acting as if he is a victim to the entire situation, taking no responsibility, and providing long-winded justifications. While difficult to listen to, these are signs that they are hurting. Neither feels understood and both feel frustrated and defeated.

As I sit and listen to them, I see it clearly. They need to break this sequence, and they need to figure out how to redistribute the physical and mental load of having a life together more equitably.

I pause for a moment and then ask them to take a pause too. "I know you're both hurting. And, the way you are talking about this right now is not helping. What research tells us is that when couples follow this sequence—criticism followed by defensiveness—they grow further and further apart. Can I help you do it another way?"

Lina and Shaun look at me with pursed lips. *Okay, tough customers*, I think. I drop my head to the side, take a deep breath, and smile gently. I want them to know I am on their side, that I understand, and that I believe it can get better . . . but the experience in my own personal life is making me question this.

"I know, this is frustrating. Let's just try it a little differently though, okay?"

They both nod their heads at me from across the room.

"Lina, you've got something important to say to Shaun, but you keep losing him as your listener because of the way you're saying it. I am going to help you share your message—*the same message*—so that he can hear it. Okay?"

Lina nods and takes a deep breath. I recognize this is hard for her, but I need her to work on changing the pattern, or we aren't going to get anywhere.

"Can you give me an example?" Lina asks.

"Of course. I want you to turn to Shaun and say something like, 'I noticed that when you took on more work hours, I felt really frustrated. I still feel really frustrated. I need input into your work schedule. Can we think through whether or not these hours are reasonable for our family together?'"

I am asking Lina to be vulnerable. This is hard work even on the best of days, but especially hard when you're upset with the person you're sharing with. I'm confident, though, that if Lina can share from her heart, she will have a better shot at getting Shaun to listen.

Lina rubs her fingers across the brown fabric couch and looks up toward the window. She stares at the blue sky and cityscape for a moment and then takes a deep breath.

"Shaun, when I found out you took more hours last week without asking me, I felt heartbroken. Truly. I know Liz said 'frustrated' but that actually wasn't it. I was heartbroken. I felt betrayed. Now, I feel mad. But really at the bottom of it, I am heartbroken. I need us to collaborate on these types of things. I need influence into how our lives are impacted by big change. I cannot carry all of this anymore. Can we please talk about your work schedule and can you let me know that there's room for me to give feedback?"

Wow, good job, Lina, I think, as I smile at her, ready to let her know she has done well. Before I can say a word though, Shaun blurts out, "Are you kidding me? How do you expect to stay home with the kids if I am not working? Do you understand what my boss is like? Influence? I give you influence over everything—there is no influence to be had with my boss. I really can't keep . . ."

As Shaun talks, he loses Lina a little more. She crosses her arms and turns her head to look in the opposite direction. She's biting her lip and holding back tears. I feel myself becoming tense and holding back my own tears as I can so deeply relate to their predicament.

"Shaun, I want to help you. What you're doing right now isn't working. Take a deep breath and look at Lina. What do you notice?"

"She's looking away."

"Right . . . so nothing you're saying right now is going in. I notice myself having to take deep breaths as I listen. This means that I am also at risk of not hearing what you have to say. I know that you've got a lot you want Lina to understand, but the way you're sharing it isn't getting that across."

He inhales deeply and looks at me.

"Yeah, I see that too. It's kind of how it is in our life in general."

"Okay, so while Lina gets critical, you get defensive. But Lina wasn't critical this time. Lina was clear and vulnerable. You need to work on taking responsibility for your part and actually understanding what she is saying before diving into your rebuttal. Can I try to help you with that?"

"I know I'm always the problem. Everything I do is wrong."

"Shaun, stay with me. It's not about you being wrong. Can you try?"

Shaun gives me a nod.

I spend time empathizing with Shaun—I know he is working hard for his family. He is worried about their finances, worried about his relationship, and trying so incredibly hard. But he isn't drowning yet; his wife is. And I need to get him to help her stay afloat.

Although I had just read the comic strip that morning, I pull out my phone and pull it up.

"Lina and Shaun, can you take a look at this for me? Does any of it resonate?"

They quietly hold my phone between them, looking at what I've pulled up. Lina smiles and peeks at Shaun to see his reaction. "Yeah," he says. "Ugh, man," he starts to rub his hands through his hair. "Okay, Lina . . . you're right. I haven't been taking enough of a role at home. It's not fair. And I get why you're so upset about it."

Instead of pointing fingers at each other—*making each other the problem*—Lina and Shaun leave the session on a path that points to the actual problems they need to solve, starting with navigating the way they distribute the load of family life.

Over the next several months, they work together to identify the tasks it takes to run their home and the level of energy needed to keep it all going. They list out what needs to be done daily, monthly, and yearly, and consciously assign roles to each other. This helps them to know who is responsible for what and relieves a large burden for them both.

Later that afternoon, Andrew and I are driving together in the car. As I sit in the passenger seat, a long list of tasks that need to be done before Monday starts rattling around in my mind: *Nola, our dog, needs to be groomed, but before she can, she has to get a vaccine. I need to make both appointments. I haven't called Aetna yet to see what is going on with the denied claim related to my C-section. We keep forgetting to replace the lightbulbs in the basement so I can never do laundry at night. We are out of detergent. I think I forgot to empty the dryer filter.*

I stop myself and look over at my husband.

"Can I read you something?" I ask.

"Sure."

For the third time that day, I open my phone to the comic strip and describe each frame to him as he drives. "That's how I feel, babe. It's making me so angry."

He looks at me with gentle eyes and squeezes my thigh. "I'm sorry. That isn't right. I am going to work on it. One thing I'd like to add," he says, "is that while I think this is a big part, I also think we just have too much on our plate in general."

"You're probably right."

I lean my head against the headrest and close my eyes, feeling relaxed for the first time in a long time.

And just as I'm about to drift to sleep, Andrew lovingly pats my escalator knee. I wince, and just like that, I'm awake again.

THE THERAPIST HEADS TO THERAPY

It's 4:00 am and I'm rocking back-and-forth, back-and-forth in the chair in George's room. He's been crying off and on for hours and no matter what I do, he still doesn't go to sleep. At five months old, people have had many hypotheses for why he cries so much—my let-down is too fast, he isn't getting enough food, his days and nights are mixed up, I'm overstimulating him during the day, I am understimulating him during the day, he is too tired, he is not tired enough.

Regardless, I've been rocking back-and-forth, back-and-forth in this chair for months. And tonight, I've started to think that maybe it would be better if I died.

I am taken aback at how matter-of-fact my thinking is on the subject. *I could put the baby in his crib and jump out of the window.* The window is only one story up, but I'm not thinking about how I'd likely only get a broken leg. I am just thinking I would like to die and that perhaps that is one easy way to do it. And if I don't die, at least I get some sleep in a hospital bed.

I am a sorry excuse for a mother anyway—my child doesn't seem bonded to me, and I have no clue how to soothe him. On top of it, I am struggling in the one area I've always excelled in: work. And my husband seems disinterested in me.

I'm nothing.

A part of me understands that these thoughts are wrong, so I get up from the chair, put George in his crib, and walk into our bedroom. "Andrew, I want to kill myself."

He looks at me, unsure of what to do. I get into our bed and fall asleep.

The next morning, I have a session with a therapist I have seen for a few weeks. Kellie is a calm woman around the same age as me. She is a kind but private therapist. I try to get to know more about her, but she never shares much with me. She's mysterious, wise, and comforting.

I had suicidal thoughts the night before, but I feel better now and would rather talk about the conflict I have with my husband, so I don't mention it.

"I know I need to learn to not be so critical," I say, as I try to untangle George's little fingers from my hair while sitting on her gray couch. As a couples therapist, I know that criticism along with defensiveness, stonewalling, and contempt are markers of the end times of a relationship.

In John Gottman's work, he found that couples who do these four things, which he dubbed the four horsemen (a play on the biblical four horsemen of the apocalypse), are on the wrong path.[2] The more chronic the behavior, the more likely the divorce.

Criticism isn't the same as giving feedback. Instead, it's when there is a problem in your life or relationship and you make that problem about the character of your partner. You can catch yourself being critical if you use the words *always* or *never* or start your sentence with *you*, as in, "You never help with anything around the house!" The first issue with bringing up problems in a critical way is that you're moving the spotlight away from the problem. Once your partner feels spotlighted, they are more likely to get defensive. At which point, round and round you go with no good outcome.

Defensiveness, then, is a reaction to believing your character is being attacked. Real or perceived criticism causes almost anyone to respond in a self-protective way. This looks like justifying your behavior before hearing its impact, explaining away your choices without taking accountability for them, or cross-criticizing to deflect. While the strategy is self-protective, it's destructive to the relationship—nothing gets resolved and resentment grows.

Stonewalling is exactly what it sounds like—becoming a stone wall in the face of conflict with your partner. You might be in the same room, but you seem very far away. You might not say much, look away, and cross your arms over your chest. When people stonewall, it's usually because they're overwhelmed. They are worried that there is nothing they can say to make it better.

Lastly, contempt is criticism, supercharged. Not only do you attack the character of your partner, you attack their worthiness. When people show contempt, they take a one-up position; and sarcasm, sneers, and put-downs get thrown around like emotional knives, causing deep wounds. Contempt is harmful, and when it is chronic, it has a high correlation with divorce.[3]

Each of these communication habits starts a cascade of distance between two people and, over time, makes it less and less likely they'll solve their problems.

So when I tell Kellie how contemptuous and critical I am, I expect her to admonish me.

Kellie doesn't do that. Instead, she says, "I dunno, maybe there is something to criticize about him. Why should it be okay for you to do all of that work while he watches TV? Why is it okay that you've cut back on your hours at work and he comes home from the office whenever he wants? Maybe he needs you to get loud and mad."

Oof... you've never studied relationships... have you Kellie? I think. Each time I have a session with Kellie, I leave feeling understood and relieved. But I also feel concerned that she is over-empathizing with me and potentially leading me astray—almost hinting that I should divorce my husband.

Similar to a lot of self-help books and share-worthy social media posts, Kellie seems to be shouting, "Love yourself!" without really taking into consideration whether I am being loving toward others too. I understand the gas-mask concept, "Put your mask on before putting anyone else's on," but I am worried it's being taken to an extreme—that I'm not being challenged and that relational intelligence is being atrophied in preference of self-preservation.

Before my appointment, I had a meeting with a lactation consultant. The issue with breastfeeding George isn't that I have a low supply; it is that my supply comes out too quickly and I am quite literally choking him while he is trying to eat. "It's okay! George and you will learn to work through this together," the consultant said. *Okay*, I thought, *keep choking my baby with breastmilk in order to feed him. Got it.*

I'm wearing a black T-shirt and it's soaked in putrid-smelling breast milk. No matter how often I change these damn nursing pads, they never absorb enough. I am so exhausted and depressed that I don't even care.

"I hate breastfeeding so much," I say to Kellie, in tears. "And I hate that consultant."

Kellie looks at me and says, "Well, why are you doing something you hate?"

"Because I have to. It's the best thing to do for George. It isn't about me."

"But it is about you. Your relationship with George is about both of you. Also, you're depressed. I don't think you are telling me how you actually feel, but I am worried about you."

"I just think I'll be judged if I quit," I say, brushing off her comment about depression. "I don't want to be judged. And I don't even understand how formula works anyway—do I just give him any type?"

"The fact you don't know how formula works is a problem. Did the hospital not give you the option?" Kellie says with a furrowed brow.

"No. They never even mentioned it. Only breastfeeding. And the lactation consultant told me to keep trying when I asked for formula information."

Kellie leans forward and looks directly at me to punctuate that she is about to make an important point. "Liz, you are depressed, exhausted, angry with your husband, and struggling to bond with your baby . . . all of this so you can breastfeed. Is it really giving you the outcome they are selling you? Is this stress worth it?"

I know Kellie is onto something, but it's so hard to accept. I've absorbed the "breast is best" mantra for so long now that it's hard to change my mind. Kellie is helping me use a tool called reality checking, where you think through the reality of a situation instead of only responding to your own long-held beliefs or emotional responses.

After the session, I go home and mentally repeat the steps of all the nights before: breastfeed (and, apparently, choke the baby with my g-force breastmilk), drink water, pump breast milk, refrigerate milk, clean the pump, cry, repeat.

Tonight though, my husband walks into the room and says, "You can't do this anymore. It's just not good for your mental health. I am going to the store and I am getting formula."

My husband, who was adopted, points out that neither of us was breastfed as a baby. And we are no worse for it. "Aha!" I say. "That must be what's been wrong with me all these years." I think I'm funny. Andrew pretends to be amused.

He leaves our house and runs around town looking for a twenty-four-hour CVS. Meanwhile, I reflect on how quickly my feelings about our marriage change—I go from thinking things are terrible to thinking we are the very best match for each other.

Shortly after, he comes home with six types of formula. "I'll look up the best way to introduce this to him," he says.

"You know what, you don't need to. We've got this."

I fill a bottle with formula and take it upstairs to George. For the first time since birth, he eats without crying and choking and fighting. And then something magical happens, he falls asleep.

I know exactly how to feed my baby, I think. *It's just not with my breast.* In that moment, my relationship to parenting starts to improve as I realize the most important experts in the room are my husband and me.

I have come to the conclusion that most of my distress is either coming from a lack of help or from following anyone and everyone's stressful advice. I think back to my session with Kellie. She was right—under my criticism was my anger. And my anger was telling me that something needed to change. So tonight Andrew and I work as a team to face what is causing the issue and improve our circumstances together.

I start thinking about all of the ways my family and I are suffering due to "best practices." The books and forums I had read on parenting, relationships, and family life were actually making it worse for me and many of my clients.

Over the coming days, I start reaching out to my friends who have children. I text my best friend Amy, "Do you think the parenting books you read were helpful or unhelpful?" and she responds, "Wildly unhelpful. Made me feel anxious. But not even just the books, those online forum posts are awful. So much pressure and judgment."

When I ask another friend, Lisa, what she thinks about all of the advice she received, she responds, "It nearly led me to a divorce. It's all so unrealistic."

And another friend said, "I feel I can never win. I don't want to go back to work, but then I get advice that it will be bad for my self-esteem if I stay home with the kids for too long. I know if I went back to work, I would be told I should be home."

Googling every single thing is driving us all mad.

GETTING TO SAFETY

By this point, I had identified two major stressors that were impacting not only my family life, but also the family life of my friends and clients: the unequal distribution of mental load and over-the-top pressure to live up to other people's standards.

As time went on, I started to notice more and more the ways in which family life was being negatively impacted by the pressures of the outside world, often made worse by the internal desire to "do it right." Everywhere I looked, people were being told what to do. All the advice givers had become dogmatic and there was a huge loss of nuance. The adage, "If it ain't broke, don't fix it," seemed lost upon these gurus of the world—instead, every message seemed to be, "It's all broken and here are a million fixes."

It's already hard enough to work a job, raise a kid, and connect with a partner. I was internalizing these voices and everything was becoming harder. And, why were the people around me dismissing the stress I was feeling and actually encouraging actions that led to more of it?

Imagine you and your partner are sitting in a canoe on a lake. It is a beautiful day—the sun is shining and you're warm and at peace. You're in a really nice canoe. It is new and shiny and has great buoyancy.

As the day goes on, this metaphorical canoe starts to go through some things. First, it hits a rock and gets the tiniest hole. It's not so bad to deal with one hole. You are happy, it's a nice day, and as water very slowly seeps into the canoe, you keep on top of it by dumping it back into the lake. However, as the day goes on, the canoe continues to fall apart. Keeping the water out is demanding more resources than you and your partner have. The holes become bigger and the canoe begins to disintegrate into a Swiss-cheese canoe. No matter how hard you work together, it becomes harder and harder to keep the canoe afloat. Your canoe starts to sink and you both start to panic. How do you react? Do you fight each other? Flee from each other? Completely freeze? Ideally, you work together to solve the problem so you can both get out safely.

Our relationships are like these canoes. Over time, stressors like mental load inequities, finances, family life, work, health, and the pressures of society start to poke holes in the canoe. The more holes we have the harder it is to keep up. And as that happens, most people respond by either having a go at each other, abandoning each other, or doing nothing at all.

The goal, though, is to learn how to look at all of the holes and work together to figure out how to get to safety.

SESSION NOTES:

In this session, we explored the mental load, the four horsemen, and reality checking. Use the following interventions to address these areas in your own life. The mental load is the invisible, intangible tasks involved in running a household.

1. INTERVENTION: IDENTIFY YOUR OWN MENTAL LOAD

Below are the categories of mental load. Take a moment to write down what you did this week in each category.

Remembering

This is the work of remembering that you need to call the dentist, RSVP to a wedding, and pick up the shirts from the dry cleaner.

Researching

This is the work of finding out how to best navigate a challenging parenting situation, how to pay your taxes, and what to do the next time you and your partner fight.

Worrying

This is the work of holding onto the worries of the family: "If we don't register for soccer camp on time, we might not get a spot," or "If we forget to make that deposit to the bank today, our account will be overdrawn next week."

Delegating

This is the work of noticing what needs to be done and asking others to do it.

After writing your list, notice what you think about it. Does it feel like a fair distribution? Unfair? Take a moment to jot down your thoughts.

2. INTERVENTION: IDENTIFY AND CHANGE THE FOUR HORSEMEN

Since the 1970s, Gottman has been studying couples. He found in his research that the communication habits he dubbed the four horsemen were responsible for unhappy marriages. In fact, people who chronically use these communication habits are more likely to divorce. The four horsemen are criticism, defensiveness, stonewalling, and contempt.

If you start getting critical, try this instead:

- Describe what you notice.

- Describe how you feel about that.

- Describe what you need.

   Example:

   "I've noticed that at the end of the day, I am often working on tasks around the house. I feel frustrated and exhausted by this. I need us to come up with a more equitable plan."

If you tend to get defensive, try this instead:

- Be short and brief in your response.

- Validate the other person's reality.

- Take responsibility.

   Examples:

   "That sounds fair."

   "You're right. You do a lot around the house at night."

   "I am not carrying my weight. I could absolutely do more."

If you tend to stonewall, try this instead:

- Ask for a break (you're overwhelmed and need space to calm down).

Examples:

"I am having a hard time talking; I need a break."

"I can't share my thoughts clearly right now. Can we come back to this tomorrow?"

"I need some time to think on this. It's important to me and we can come back to it."

If you tend to show contempt, try this instead:

- Start noticing your emotions over the week and practice labeling them.

- When you have feelings of rage or resentment, take a pause before speaking.

- Try to narrate your thoughts and actions instead of belittling your partner.

Examples:

"I feel rage right now."

"I am thinking that I really want to scream at you right now, but I know I need to walk away."

3. INTERVENTION: REALITY CHECKING

Reality checking is a common therapy intervention that helps people see a situation for what it really is, rather than what one fears it might be. It helps us to distinguish our inner turmoil from what's actually happening.

If you're experiencing inner turmoil that is adding stress to your life, take a moment to follow these steps:

Work toward flexible thinking. Do this by pushing yourself to have what is called helpful other thoughts. Don't let the "helpful" part make you believe they all need to be positive. Helpful other thoughts aren't about positive thinking; they are about expanded thinking. When we have inner turmoil due to stress, some of it is related to rigid thinking about how we are supposed to respond to the stress.

Thanks to Kellie, I worked on developing more flexible, less shame-based thinking around my struggles with breastfeeding. To have helpful other thoughts, first write down your own automatic distressing thoughts. Mine were: *Mothers should breastfeed because it is best for the baby, and if I stop, people will judge me.*

Then, starting with the word *maybe*, come up with other possible thoughts, truths, and scenarios around the same subject. Set a timer and try to come up with as many other thoughts as you can:

- Maybe breastfeeding is really great for other people and not for me.

- Maybe my baby hates breast milk even though other babies prefer it.

- Maybe my baby will be happier once they have formula.

- Maybe my baby will hate the formula and I will need to find another solution.

- Maybe my baby will be less healthy if I keep pushing breastfeeding since he isn't eating enough.

- Maybe I will continue to be depressed if I don't begin to use formula.

- Maybe I can use formula *and* breastfeed.

By taking time to expand the possibilities, you are recognizing that the way you are thinking or feeling is not the only way to think or feel in the situation. In pushing myself to think other thoughts, I was able to recognize that my rigid thinking was causing me more distress than the reality of the situation. These new thoughts freed me to address feeding in a more flexible way.

Notice your emotions and distinguish them from facts. You might be afraid, nervous, angry, or sad. When you can name your feelings, you can lean into the emotional experience you are having. You can combine that with the flexible thinking you worked on in step 1 to honor your feelings while still opening up to other possibilities. For example, "The reality is that I am sad that I can't breastfeed comfortably, *and* there are many ways for mothers to feed and bond with their baby and still be okay." Note that just because I was sad did not mean that there was nothing else I could do about the situation. It was okay for me to feel sad *and* also begin to consider other options.

Ask for outside perspectives. Go to other trusted people and hear what they have to say about the situation. Ask them to be as objective as possible. By allowing myself to listen to my husband, Kellie, and my friends, I could see that there were many ways to think about my situation. This allowed me to wade through the options to find what worked best for me.

When we are stressed, we become myopic. Reality checking helps us to see that there is often more than one way to do something within our lives and that we can experience our feelings about it while still allowing ourselves to switch gears if needed.

Think about your own stressors. Is there one you could practice reality checking with? Your biggest task here is to make the thoughts you're having about your stressor more flexible.

As you think about the things driving you crazy in life, how much of it is coming from expectations you've set for yourself based on outside pressures?

CHAPTER 2

Shine a Light on Your Stressors

S hortly after George is born, I know things aren't okay between Andrew and I, so I schedule a couples therapy appointment with a woman who has an office close to our home. Andrew is uncomfortable with the idea. To him, needing a therapist to help solve our problems means that something is very wrong with us. He agrees only because I am relentless in asking him to go.

On our way to the office, we get a little lost, which makes us late. It's close to our house, but on a strange street. Andrew, who is already frustrated about giving an hour of his evening to what he considers an unhelpful endeavor, is now more irritated because Siri is sending us in circles. I sit in the passenger seat biting my lip. I just want this to go well, but I can already tell that it isn't going to.

We finally find parking in a lot a few blocks away and dart across a busy street to get to the front door. I look at my watch. We are five minutes late for a forty-five-minute appointment. Then, I look up at the door. A sign on printer paper reads, "Use the back door please."

Damn it, I think. We both look at each other, take a deep breath, and head around to the back of the building. After what seems like an endless circle of hallways, we find our way to a brightly lit waiting room.

"Liz? Andrew?"

We nod our heads.

"Follow me this way," she says, pointing to a door down another hallway.

We walk into the office and Andrew immediately starts talking . . . and I can't get a word in.

As I listen to him, my thoughts start to swirl. I have a million words in my mind, and at the same time I feel there is nothing I can say that would make a difference. The longer I sit quietly, the more my ears ring. *I am never going to get a chance to share*, I think. And even if I do, not much will come out clearly. As I think about this, I am flooded with all of the things that won't improve if I don't get a chance to speak. Inside, my mind is busy, but on the outside, I feel absolutely frozen. Andrew keeps talking, but I can't process what is he is saying. I sit quietly and very still.

While Andrew talks and I sit frozen, the therapist tries to teach us some things. Here and there her voice makes its way through my mental chatter. I hear her say things like:

"Liz, don't you want to talk?" I shake my head no.

And:

"Andrew, it seems like you are feeling defensive. Sometimes that happens if you think someone is criticizing you."

And:

"I think the two of you would be in a better place if you could practice this speaking and listening skill. Let me tell you about it."

I feel so overwhelmed. I understand what she is saying; they are things I tell my couples too, but none of them seem to be helping in the moment.

At the end of the session, I feel defeated. I smile at her as we walk out. Andrew doesn't even look her way. I think she gave him feedback that didn't land well. His jaw is tense and my shoulders are slumped. We get into the car and don't say a word. It takes us about an hour to feel calm in our bodies again. The session was a flop.

To this day, I still can't even remember the therapist's name, let alone the assessment she gave us at the end of the session. That makes sense— when people are overwhelmed, it's hard to retain information.

The morning after our session, I reflect on what went wrong. Why couldn't we communicate with each other? I'm a therapist for goodness' sake. And yet, everything I knew, I couldn't do.

Later, I would come to realize that the therapist was making a common mistake—she talked to us as if we were in our safe brain and body, but we weren't. We were fearful about the state of our relationship, and our bodies were in a state of stress. This state of stress created a physiological overwhelm that made it difficult for us to process information and communicate the way we would have under the best of circumstances.

WHAT IS STRESS?

When couples come to see me, I'll ask, "What do you think is going on?" And most will respond with some form of, "We've got communication issues." "Okay," I'll respond. "And what does 'communication issues' mean?"

From here, I'll receive a variety of answers. A few sound a little like this:

- "We yell at each other."

- "We can't make decisions."

- "We never talk."

- "My partner doesn't know how to share their feelings. They block me out."

To understand more, I will ask them why they think this is. Often, this results in a blame game. "Well, it's not me . . . it's them." They go on to share a laundry list of issues. "I think they've never processed their childhood issues," or "They have an avoidant personality," or "They are just plain-old lazy."

It would be easy to take these answers at face value, and sometimes that is all that is needed. But often, I find that the yelling or withdrawing, the gridlock, or the lack of emotional intimacy is only the tip of the iceberg.

It is certainly what you see—how could you not see the blatant behaviors that hurt so much? But these behaviors might be a symptom, not a cause.

Often couples yell and freeze up and disconnect because they are stuck in a constant stress loop. Stress loops start when something—an event, smell, touch, taste, sound, or belief—activates the stress response.

These stressors are either internal—self-criticism and internalized worries, for example—or external—the fight you had with your partner earlier in the day or the update you just saw on the most recent world crisis.

When your stress response is activated by one of these things, your body begins a neurological and hormonal physiological process. It starts to prepare itself to protect you from threats and keep you alive by changing the way it operates. It's an evolutionary process that, unfortunately for our relationships, hasn't been updated since the days we were trying to outrun lions.

Whether you're coming face-to-face with a lion or feeling like your partner is making a bad decision that will negatively impact you, your body will go through the same stress response cycle to varying degrees. It does so by pushing blood to your muscles to get them ready to work hard, increasing your heart rate so you can run more quickly, and releasing endorphins so that your body is numb to whatever it is you need to do to survive. You gain an increased focus on survival and tune out whatever else is going on.

Based on what the threat is, what your options are, and who you are, your body might utilize hormones and neurological processes to make you fight, flee, or freeze.

If the lion is chasing you, your breathing will increase so you can run and you'll push through the pain of running so fast and so long. You will be hyper-focused on getting to a safe destination. That means, if you pass something that you'd otherwise be interested in, you're not going to even notice it.

This process became obvious to me when I was twenty-one years old and accidentally slammed a sliding glass door on my finger at a party. Although my finger had been severed by the door, I continued talking to my friend on the porch until she pointed out that blood was pumping out of my hand and I was missing a finger. When I registered the threat, I went into a flee response. Even though I was bleeding profusely and missing a finger, I could still use my hand. I didn't notice the pain. I worked to pull open the heavy door and directed people—"Get a sock! Now! Give me a hairband now!"—as we wrapped my finger and stopped the bleeding by tying it off tightly. I grabbed my friend's keys and pushed her out the door so she could drive me to the hospital. Everything was in slow motion. I was focused, but only on getting myself to safety.

When people later shared the things that were going on around me during the incident, I didn't remember any of it at all. The reactions of the other people, the blood on the door, the route we took to the hospital.

That's because not only does the body prime itself to get to safety, but it also starts to shut down processes that you don't really need in the moment. Memory is reduced as are interpersonal skills. Your digestion slows down and your immune function is impacted. Your body reserves all the energy that it would utilize elsewhere to keep you safe.

In both examples above, the physiological process makes sense. There is a life-or-death threat—you need to get away from the lion or you've got to stop the bleeding—and you need your stress response to kick into gear to keep you safe.

But when our stress response starts playing out over and over again in daily life, it becomes problematic to our own health and to our relationships—neither of which can thrive in a constant stress state.

Enter the reason for this book—people are navigating constant stressors and living in stressed states, and because of this, relationships are floundering. The more stressed you are, the more you lose your ability to express your thoughts and feelings, show humor, solve problems, and offer affection. You can see how this would result in the described problem behaviors listed above.

Not everyone has the same stress response. Some people become agitated. They get short and ill-tempered. They become loud and grouchy. Others become cold and withdrawn. They get quiet. They freeze up. They become passive and absent. And when two are doing a tango to the tune of stress it becomes especially complicated to discuss complex issues, explore differences of opinion, and come to consensus.

When people are in a non-stress state they are "at rest." They are able to do the things we should be able to do when at rest—play, dream, converse, hug, plan, and so forth.

When people are in a stressed state, they might no longer be able to do these things. This might seem like your brain isn't "functioning" at its top capability. However, it's doing exactly what it *should* be doing in response to whatever stress it is sensing.

If the lion is chasing you, should you really be chit chatting with the neighbor?

Or, if you are worried you won't be able to make next month's rent and are at risk of homelessness, is your brain really going to dedicate precious resources to communicating with your partner about the vacation they've been dreaming up?

Stress is the body's response to a challenge. Sometimes these are positive challenges—this is called eustress. Pushing yourself a little harder at the gym, trying a new hobby, putting yourself out there on Bumble to make a new friend. All of this is challenging but *positive* stress that helps you make forward movement in your life.

Sometimes stress is the result of feeling pain, uncertainty, or just "too much" of something. This could be too much eustress—working too hard at the gym, spending too much money on a hobby—or too much distress—like hearing bad news about your health, losing a job, or fear over your financial future.

Fortunately for us, our body is miraculous. It manages an expansive world that not only keeps us alive but also allows us to do the things that make living so special.

Unfortunately for us, the stressed body does not always respond to what is actually happening in the moment. Instead, it uses its archive of stored information from our life to make faster-than-the-speed-of-light decisions. A childhood experience with a parent who got loud when they were angry might cause our hearts to race when we're around someone who is a loud talker in adulthood. Because of those quicker-than-lightening thoughts, when we are stressed, we can rapidly judge our partner in the wrong way.

Take the following story: It's getting dark and Arianna is running as fast as she can down the street. Her heart is racing. Her ankle hurts, but she can't stop now. She has to keep going. She looks behind her to see if she's in the clear yet . . .

As you're reading this, what are you feeling? Which pieces of the story has your brain filled in? Where is she running to? Why is she looking behind her? Clear of what?

As I wrote that story, I thought of Arianna running a marathon. She's so close to the end, it's getting dark, and her body is tired. Her ankle hurts, but she has to keep going. She looks behind her to see if she's gotten far enough ahead of her friendly rival. Maybe you assumed the same storyline, maybe you didn't. Whatever your brain put together is due to your life experiences or your exposure, personality, or thinking patterns.

This same thing happens when you are interacting with the world. Sometimes, the meaning you derive is accurate—the tone of the email *does* mean you're going to be fired and the way that your partner looked at you when you shared a new idea *does* mean they disapprove.

It makes sense then that our brains would try to prime us to avoid danger, *Don't open the email! You're not ready to be fired!* Or to attack it, *Stomp into that office right now and tell your boss you quit so they can't fire you first!*

However, there are times when your brain is mislabeling the situation. Perhaps you've known someone in the past who used that tone when you were about to be punished, but this particular boss is just fairly dry and direct in emails. Maybe there is a type of glance that symbolized disapproval in your childhood, but for your partner, it just means they are thinking.

When you start to experience stress, the complex brain puts together many different signals and observations that lead it to believe you are doing something challenging, which could be dangerous, and so it needs to be alert to help you out.

The observations it's making have to do with every part of your system—your breathing, digestion, muscle function, heart function, skin, and so forth.

Think back to the last time you were in a stressful situation. You might remember that it became harder to talk. Many couples will describe feeling like their words are "at the tip of their tongue" but they are unable to articulate them. Or, sometimes, talking becomes too easy. People will say whatever comes to mind with no filter when they're overstimulated. They will experience many rapid thoughts and emotions, but won't be able to integrate them in a way that allows for problem-solving or communication.

If you notice that you're struggling to communicate effectively, having a difficult time processing information, or feel as if all the sounds around you are extra loud or muted, then it might mean your nervous system is responding to what it considers a worrisome, overly challenging situation.

As our brain develops, we do something called tuning and pruning—we continue to fine-tune which stimuli symbolize safety or danger, and we continue to prune those that do not.[1] This mostly happens in childhood but can continue into adulthood if we make a conscious effort.

When your assumption is wrong, you can "prune" by pushing yourself to respond in ways you usually wouldn't if you were in danger—taking a brief moment for a deep inhale or asking to hold your partner's hand, for example.

When it's right, you can "tune" by having self-compassion. "I am so overwhelmed right now. This stress is trying to get me to take care of myself. I am going to listen to it."

Now, let's imagine that this situation is not just momentary. It isn't the tone of an email or a quick glance; it's being fired and not being able to find a job. It's living with someone who frequently puts you down and discourages you. Your distressed state will be more than momentary—it might become chronic.

When people get to this point, almost anything can be sensed as a danger cue. This leads to less cooperation and more self-focus. You might notice that your emotions are hard to regulate, so much so that even when you "tell yourself to stop," you can't. Perhaps you'll even have a dialogue with yourself, *Why am I screaming like this? I need to stop!* And yet you'll find you can't stop yourself at all.

Under chronic stress, humans live in a flooded, dysregulated state that causes challenges with impulse control and the awareness of others. People under chronic stress do things like put people down and get defensive. They struggle to listen, show empathy, or see nuance.

Throughout this process, we become what others might see as more chaotic and less like ourselves, but in reality, this is just our inner survivor coming out.

Consider the COVID-19 era, when our society became increasingly polarized. In therapy sessions, I listened as people, almost overnight, disowned family members, ended friendships, or bullied strangers online due to differences in their reaction to the virus. "'Til Stress Do Us Part" could be a good title for the time, when we all became more and more separate from each other—physically, emotionally, and relationally.

It was a time of very little empathy, listening, and nuance.

People are still recovering today from the ways in which they hurt each other. While some feel righteous, many feel regret and guilt about their own behavior or anger and their indignation about the behavior of others.

Yet all of this behavior was totally predictable and absolutely human. When we are in survival mode, we are primed to find the threats and protect ourselves from them. Unfortunately, when we are especially stressed, we see even slight differences in opinion as a threat.

This makes it difficult to problem solve, negotiate, or find common ground. According to Roy Baumeister of the University of Queensland, "in their natural state, people make compromises very effectively . . . But when resources are low, they stop compromising."[2]

This is also what happens in our homes. Couples under significant stress can struggle to respond cooperatively with each other. Once they reach their coping threshold, individuals tend to have a primary stress response type: the venomous king cobra, the fearful deer, or the opossum, playing dead.

If you're the king cobra when stressed you might lash out, become critical or contemptuous, and be easy to agitate. In a partnership, this might look like someone who yells or complains about their partner. During daily tasks, they might be someone who curses out a customer service agent. And at work, you can become confrontational with your colleagues.

If you relate to the fearful deer, you might notice yourself thinking of your exit as soon as there is conflict. Perhaps if you sense your boss is upset with you, you consider quitting instead of hashing it out. At home, when in an argument, you might stomp out of the room or rapidly change the subject.

And, if you tend to play dead, like the opossum, you likely withdraw when things get tough. You might ignore the pile of bills on the counter, clam up and stonewall during tough conversations, or ignore your boss's emails.

If you relate to all of these, it's likely that they happen in relation to each other. Perhaps first you are the deer, but when triggered further, become the cobra. Maybe when the venom doesn't keep the predator at bay, you play dead like the opossum.

Just like the cobra, deer, and opossum, we are animals. And we have instincts that come out when we are afraid. However, unlike those animals, we have the human capacity to better understand our reactions and work toward building awareness and self-soothing behaviors to become cooperative, even when it's hard.

Couple Profile

Neira (29/F) and Jon (35/M) have been dating for two years and are cohabitating in the city. Neira is in law school and Jon works as a traveling consultant. Neira and Jon come to therapy because they are having trouble making decisions together.

When Neira and Jon visited me for their first appointment, they were both under tremendous amounts of stress. Jon's nephew and brother had recently died in a car accident, and he was traveling weekly for work and experiencing chronic illness. Neira's father had died earlier in the year, and she was studying for the bar exam and had a significant amount of debt.

They also had a lot of decisions to make. Should Jon change his job to be home more often? Do they move so that Neira can be closer to her grieving mother? Do they combine their bank accounts even though Neira is carrying so much debt?

It's been four sessions now, and whenever Jon and Neira try to talk about any one of these issues, they become combative with each other. Rather than responding empathetically to Neira's tears regarding how important it is to her to live closer to her mother, Jon becomes argumentative and difficult to talk to. He turns his body away from Neira, rolls his eyes, and says cutting things. A king cobra in action.

When Jon tries to share with Neira his fears about money, Neira starts to cry, and then when she feels too overwhelmed, she shuts down completely. Her inner opossum comes out.

I hope that today's session will be different, but I don't think it will. Neira comes in as she always does—enthusiastically. She is vibrant and sweet and bounces across my office, almost jumping on the couch when she arrives. She has a childlike presence to her—in the best way—as she kicks off her shoes and folds her feet underneath her.

Jon walks in slowly, finding a spot to sit at the far end of the couch. Reserved and serious, it's hard to read Jon when he comes in. From my individual sessions with him, I know there is a gentle core, but I haven't seen him use it with Neira.

"How are you both doing?" I ask.

Neira's expression changes. She pulls her knees into her chest and starts to cry. "It's been so hard Liz, Jon is always so mad and we can't talk about anything."

As Neira cries, Jon remains stiff. His hands are on his knees and he looks forward. He gives almost no reaction to the pain his partner is feeling. Then, he turns to her and sneers, "Really? We can't talk about anything? Then what the heck were we doing last night?"

"Jon, what's going on? Neira is sharing her concerns and is upset. I think she feels attacked and I can tell you do too." I try to empathize with both sides, hoping this might soften him. It doesn't.

Jon looks directly at me with his jaw clenched, "You know what, I'm done. You aren't helping. This is bullshit." His anger and frustration are palpable. I can tell Jon is overwhelmed.

I've seen this type of interaction many times between people who are otherwise empathetic and kind. Add a disagreement that threatens someone's sense of self or security on top of a life that is already stressful, and you're likely to see it spin out of control.

"Seriously. Why is it so fucking hard for us to just agree on things and move forward? Life is already hard enough as it is, and here we are fighting over these decisions when it's already clear what the most responsible answers are." Jon grabs his water bottle and makes a gesture as if he is about to get up and leave.

"Jon, stay with us," I say in a calm, slow voice as I reach across the room to hand him a pulse oximeter. In Gottman Method Couples Therapy, we ask couples to put pulse oximeters on their fingers to track physiological distress. A pulse oximeter tracks the heartbeats per minute of each individual. If someone's heart rate goes above one hundred beats per minute (BPM) while in the session, this is a sign to the therapist that the person is in diffuse physiological arousal, also known as flooding. We monitor this because we know that unless someone is at baseline, it can be very difficult, if not impossible, for them to communicate effectively.

"Put this on your finger."

Jon takes the pulse oximeter from my hand and places it on his finger. The numbers quickly rise and it starts to beep once they hit one hundred.

"Wow, your body is overwhelmed," I say. Jon starts to cry. I take a deep breath and count to ten. *You don't always need to say something to help someone*, I remind myself, *sometimes just being quiet and calm is enough.*

I can tell Jon's nervous system is in a dysregulated state, also known as a "flooded state." This helps me to avoid therapy interventions that might set him up for failure—like asking him to talk to Neira or show affection. At this moment, Jon can't talk, listen, accept, or show affection, so I won't ask him to.

Instead, I am going to address the physical experience he is having in his body. It's not really our thoughts about what's going on that leads us to behave reactively—it's the stimulus we are feeling in our body in response. As a therapist, I have to help Jon become aware of what is happening in his body so he understands the way it drives him to behave.

But first, I have to get Neira on board.

"Neira," I say. "I know you've got some really important things to say, and I want Jon to be able to hear you and be there for you. I have some things I want to share with you and Jon about what's going on here, but we need to take a little break first. Can you do me a favor and take this twenty-dollar bill and go grab us some coffee?"

Neira takes a deep breath and wipes her teary, blotchy face with a tissue. "Sure," she says. She looks in the mirror and pats her cheeks, trying to reduce the redness from crying. Neira is so sad and so badly wants Jon to be there for her. But she takes my advice, fixes her hair into a neat bun, and walks to the door.

"While you're out, Neira, I want you to pick one thing you are going to count. It could be clouds, cars, anything. Try to focus on counting. And as you do that breathe in and out."

I know that it isn't easy to step away from a conversation you want to have with someone. I assume Neira is probably having her own physiological response to being asked to take a break. Offering her a mindfulness activity, like counting, can help.

For a few minutes, Jon and I sit in complete silence in my dim office. I look out the window and think about my son, who is home with my husband this Saturday afternoon. I wonder what they are doing right now.

Perhaps counting clouds and cars too. I turn my attention back to Jon, tilting my head to offer a gentler glance.

Jon is leaning forward and staring into his hands, picking at his cuticles. *A good sign*, I think. *His body knows he is stressed and is working to soothe itself*. He looks up at me and tries to speak, then takes another exasperated breath. *There it is . . . another sign he is calming himself . . .* and then he says, "Yeah, I dunno. Maybe this relationship isn't meant to be."

Oof, still flooded. Jon's voice is detached. It isn't connected to what he is saying. Rather, the words represent an attempt, like picking the cuticles and taking a deep exhale, to relieve his pain and distress.

"Jon, let's not talk right now. Let's just take a moment to calm your body." I take a deep breath to calm my own body. I know that the best way to coach Jon is to be calm myself.

"I have a couple magazines. Do you want to look at one? *People*? *Cosmo*? *Psychology Today*?"

"*People* is fine."

I hand Jon the outdated *People* magazine that has been sitting on my desk. I quietly leave the room and grab him a glass of water down the hallway. I come back into the room and set the glass of water next to him.

"I am going to go to the bathroom. I'll be right back. Just drink some water and read the magazine." I dim the lights, open the window to let in some air, and walk down the hallway.

Over the years, while working with couples in dysregulated states, I have become adept at recognizing my own stress state. When my heart rate speeds up, I do a lot of work to make sure I can stay grounded and secure so that my clients can have a safe container. It wasn't always this way. In my early years, couples arguing or shutting each other out would dysregulate me. My heart would race, my ears would ring, and I'd feel overwhelmed and unsure of what to say to help them.

In those days, just like the therapist Andrew and I had met with, my work was based on dealing with the cognitive aspects of conflict— stopping the bickering cycle, pointing out the unhelpful things they said or did, and teaching them something else to say. Once I learned that much of the work is actually about soothing stress, I was able to lean into the importance of soothing my own.

In this case, while Jon yelled at me, I took deep breaths, rubbed my fingertips gently against the arm of my chair, and reminded myself that this wasn't Jon. It was Jon's reaction to stress. As I walk down the hallway to the bathroom, I feel light. My stress response hasn't kicked in because I feel safe and secure in my own body.

On my way back to the office, I run into Neira who is holding a tray with three coffees from Starbucks. "I think I remember you sharing that you like chai . . . is that right?" I smile. "Yes, I love it! Thank you so much Neira. I'm going to have you sit out here for a little longer. How about you look through a magazine and sip on your drink. We'll all come back together shortly."

After fifteen minutes, I bring Neira back into my office and we all gather again. Jon, clearly more relaxed, has his arms spread across the back of the couch. He is breathing more regularly and has a softer look on his face. He smiles when Neira hands him a pumpkin spice latte.

I can see that Jon is back with us. He is breathing, smiling, and showing playful social cues that show he is "safe and secure." It's in this zone that we can be cooperative with others.

Because I can tell that Neira and Jon are both calm, I take a moment to explain that when people are distressed, it becomes really hard to listen and show empathy to each other.

"If your partner has reached the level of distress where they can no longer communicate effectively, they are not going to be able to have a satisfactory conversation with you. It's just scientifically impossible. It's so much better to take a break—for twenty minutes or more—to self-soothe," I say.

"This is truly such a relief to hear," Neira says. "I have been feeling really defeated with how Jon and I behave. We both just get into the worst loops. This is really helping me understand, at least for myself, why I shut down and can't communicate. Jon, what do you think?"

"I agree," says Jon. "I want to be calm and collected, and I feel really ashamed when I get so mad. It's hopeful to hear that maybe there is something I can do to prevent it."

Jon and Neira's session resembles hundreds of other sessions I have had with couples in recent years. The trick is to recognize when talking isn't working, to slow down, and to figure out how to soothe each person so they feel safe and secure.

HOW TO IDENTIFY STRESS

When people become partners, they are making the decision to take on a lifetime of stress together. Inevitably, over time, many stressful events will end up impacting both people. Studies show that the stress impacting one person in a relationship spills over, not only impacting the other person, but also the functioning of the relationship.[3] That's just life. The tricky thing is that most of us don't know how to identify stress and end up conflating stress with a belief that the relationship is flawed. Because of this confusion, many couples come to therapy with a running list of issues, the most common being communication problems ("We just need to learn how to talk to each other better!") or assigning some sort of pathology to their partner ("They are so avoidant!" "They're clearly a narcissist!").

I'm no different.

Our son wasn't even one on our first wedding anniversary. We both worked full time, and each night we'd stuff our faces with whatever food we could find, clean some of the dishes, get baby bottles ready, and once George was in bed, sit on the couch and watch a show. Or at least part of a show. Most of the time, I fell asleep by the end of the opening scene, immediately after promising, "I'll stay up this time."

On our anniversary, we agreed that we would do "something special." Andrew spent time planning a Friday evening that would recreate our wedding festivities. We would eat dinner at the restaurant that hosted our rehearsal dinner and then go get drinks at Le Meridien, where we had our ceremony and reception.

Most importantly, we'd get a babysitter early enough in the day to shower, get dressed, and look nice for each other. The week leading up to our anniversary, I had every intention of getting a new outfit. But, of course, I didn't find time until Friday afternoon.

With store closing times looming, I felt an immense pressure to find something that showed Andrew I cared enough to look good for him. Rushing up and down a busy city street, I searched for something to wear—anything to wear—that would look nice. But nothing felt nice on my body, which was different than before, a fact I hadn't fully accepted. Finally, five minutes before the shops closed, I bought an overpriced pair of drawstring silk dress pants and a black turtleneck.

I rushed to my car, sat in traffic for an hour, and ran in the house to get ready. The plan to give myself an hour or two had collapsed into thirty minutes. If I didn't feel sexy that morning, I certainly didn't feel sexy that night. Rushed, tired, and uncomfortable in my own skin, I slid on the silk pants and turtleneck, stood in front of the mirror, and realized I looked like I was going on a job interview, not a date. I felt angry about how I looked; the outfit, the new weight around my hips, the dark circles under my eyes. I felt like a teenager again, back in my childhood bedroom wanting to shout, "I don't have anything to wear! I *am not* going out!"

"Liz, you ready?" Andrew shouted up the steps.

My muscles clenched, my stomach twisted into knots, and my chest rose. I was so stressed, overwhelmed, and unhappy that even being asked a simple question like "are you ready" infuriated me.

"Yeah, I guess I am ready, if we are in a rush," I said with a passive-aggressive attitude. "It's not like I ever get time to get ready anyway, so who cares. Let's go."

"Whoa, babe . . . what happened?" he asked with a surprised look on his face.

"I look terrible."

"You look great. What can we do to cheer you up?" he tried again to loosen me up.

"Nothing."

I walked down the steps with a scowl. I couldn't tell if I wanted to scream or cry.

Snap out of it, I remember telling myself. But I couldn't. I was completely snapped into my own pity party. Nothing was breaking me out of it.

As can be assumed, the night didn't end well. We ended up bickering at dinner and continued to argue over drinks. I said a lot of things I did not mean. My inner voice told me to shut up many times but I didn't listen. Alcohol and stress are not a good mix.

The next morning, I woke up in a foggy shame spiral and thought, *We really need to see a therapist again to help us communicate*. I also thought, *I never want to talk about that night again.*

What I wish I would have noticed was that it wasn't our communication that needed fixing, but our stress. I am a couples therapist. I know plenty about communication and healthy relationships, but it did not matter in that moment how much I knew about the nonviolent communication process or how clearly I understood the power of affection, humor, or play. I was so stressed—from my work, my exhaustion, and my deep unhappiness about living in my own body—that nothing other than self-soothing and co-regulation with Andrew would have allowed me to move from my wound-up position.

We didn't need to see a therapist to teach us more communication skills, we needed a therapist to help us identify our stress and learn to manage it—together and individually.

After "The Night That Shall Not Be Mentioned," Andrew and I tried couples therapy again. This time, we made an appointment with another therapist in a neighboring town. Darla's office was ten minutes away in idyllic Chestnut Hill, with its colonial-era homes and cobblestone streets. But Andrew and I were so stressed that everything about the place pissed us off.

The cobblestones meant we had to drive slowly and were going to be late. Who put their office in a spot like this?

The little town had a small amount of parking and we had to pay for it, what a rip off!

The tiny waiting room had no table; were we really supposed to sign these damn forms on our laps without a clipboard?

In a stressed state, anything and everything can be seen through the least-gracious and most-negative lens.

After a few moments of waiting, Andrew and I were asked to come back to Darla's office. Darla was my mom's age and wore the traditional therapist uniform: comfortable looking pants and an oversized, brightly patterned tunic. She looked like the type of person you'd want to have tea and biscuits with.

We spent two hours with Darla. Most of it discussing "The Night That Shall Not Be Mentioned." Then, Darla took a detour. She asked us about stress. She gave both Andrew and me paper and pens. "Write it down," she said. "Write down a list of things you are navigating in your life right now that may or may not be causing you stress."

As I started writing, I noticed a catharsis. It felt good to get this all onto paper.

"Just a quick note," Darla said in a soft voice. "Stress can be related to good things as well . . . you know holidays you're planning, purchases you are excited to make. Don't forget to include those types of things too."

My list got longer and so did Andrew's.

We both signaled we were done by setting down our pens and looking up at Darla. She reached her hand across the room, asking us to hand her our papers. She studied them for a moment and then said, "This is a lot . . ." With those words, I started to cry, first holding the tears back behind my eyeballs and then letting them drip down my face. Writing and then sharing was a release.

She continued, "I can see you are both feeling tearful about that. It's a lot, Liz and Andrew. And look, you are both loving people. I can tell you love each other very much. But if you don't figure out how to navigate all of the things on this paper, you're going to be very unhappy no matter how much we talk about your unhappiness. Get these lists under control first."

We forked over $250 and said we'd email her when we were ready to schedule our next appointment.

We didn't email. "Two-hundred-and-fifty dollars for her to tell us we're stressed?" Andrew asked.

"I know. I was expecting more from the session," I responded.

However, sometimes the right answer for change is the simplest answer for change. Darla didn't need to do anything fancy. She needed to point out our stress. And while at first, we might have brushed off her suggestion to combat it, she watered a seed that was growing, leading us toward a more manageable life.

WHEN COUPLES ARE ON DIFFERENT PAGES

"Get these lists under control," Deb's voice echoes in my mind as I prep for my next couple. Her advice is good, but I am not sure how to put it into action when I am working so much. It's a rainy Saturday morning and I am meeting with Jon and Neira again. When they arrive, though Neira is smiling, as she often does, I know that the stressors in their lives are weighing heavily on her. To Jon, it seems as if Neira doesn't care about the realities of life. She's always just "happy go lucky" and doesn't think about the broader impact of big decisions. He feels Neira doesn't take his concerns seriously enough.

But I know Neira's smile is not a symbol of happiness, rather an ode to how she deals with everything in life. Just "get through it" is her motto. *It will all be okay in the end*, she convinces herself. And, while this is true, it often erases another truth—that some things are hard and require a bit more focus.

Neira and Jon sit down on my couch, leaving enough room for one or maybe even two other people to fit between them. That's to say they are sitting very far apart.

"I'd like us to start today with an exercise, if you'd be open to it."

Neira smiles at me. Hers is genuine. She likes therapy exercises, and it is clear that she is excited to see what I will say next. Jon nods his head reluctantly.

I hand them paper and pens and ask them to list their stressors.

"All of them?" Jon smiles. "If so, you will need to give me more paper," he says with a friendly laugh.

Neira smiles and laughs at Jon's joke. "Yes, Jon will definitely need more paper," she plays.

"I've got an entire pad of paper if you need it," I say.

Jon and Neira write down their stressors.

Here's a glimpse of Jon's list:

- Scheduling upcoming work trips

- Updating auto payments to new credit card

- Taking car in to get inspected

- Dealing with leaking roof—cannot afford new roof

- Concerned about our savings account

- Researching new doctors

- Looking up debt repayment plan for Neira

- Aunt and uncle—need to support them

- Figuring out a cleaning schedule so house isn't a mess

- Do I leave my job? Interview for a new job?

- Getting flea remediation

- Can we afford to move?

Jon's list covers the front and back of his legal ruled paper. Neira's on the other hand, has one thing:

- Our relationship

While partners might live very similar lives, they can have wildly different perceptions of stressors and have differing abilities to recognize their own stress and label it as such.

Because of these differing perceptions, people tend to be unaware of the total impact. It's important to understand what is being faced and to note where it's coming from, how often it's happening, and how big the issue is.

The origin of stress within a relationship can be broken into two categories: external and internal stress. According to couples stress researcher Guy Bodenmann, external stressors are the stressors that originate outside of the relationship—a partner having an upsetting meeting with their boss, getting caught in daily traffic on the way home from work, or having a sick parent.[4]

Whereas internal stressors are things that happen within the relationship—differing ideas about which house project to take on next, opposing viewpoints about how to raise children, or sadness related to a partner's chronic illness.

Stress comes in many shapes and sizes and is categorized as either major or minor and acute or chronic. Major stressors are big events—the death of a loved one, the loss of a job, or a major move. While minor stressors are experiences like sitting on the phone for a long time with customer service or getting stuck in traffic. Chronic stress is something experienced over and over with long-lasting impacts, while acute stress is temporary and often has impacts limited to a single instance. You might experience:

- A minor stressor that is chronic:

  Having to sit on the phone every day to argue over medical bills

- A major stressor that is chronic:

  Having to go to cancer treatments multiple times a week

- A minor stressor that is acute:

  Having a phone call that is frustrating with a customer service agent

- A major stressor that is acute:

  Being stuck in a very bad storm, like a hurricane, but leaving without injury or loss

Both major and minor stressors impact relational functioning. Minor stressors, however, tend to have more opportunity for change and seem to have a bigger impact on relational functioning over time.

Minor stressors are the demands we experience that require frequent emotional and physical energy and time. Things like packing lunches for school or making medical appointments, cutting the grass or waxing the floors, and navigating workplace dilemmas like having daily conversations with a difficult colleague. While these might seem "minor," they tend to cause chronic frustration and not only change the baseline mood of the person who is experiencing the stress but also set the stage for the relationship they are in.

Major stressors, however, are related to critical, distressing, and big life events. At times, these life events are expected and difficult. Examples are:

- Spending a large sum of money on a house

- Having a baby

- Experiencing the death of a parent

There are also unexpected major stressors in life—the types of things that just *aren't* supposed to happen. These run on a spectrum from highly burdensome to highly traumatizing. Experiences like:

- Being diagnosed with cancer

- Becoming paralyzed

- Getting sued

- The death of a child

- Being mugged or robbed

Major stressors can certainly cause a lot of pain, chaos, and difficulty for a couple. However, it's the minor stressors and how they are handled in daily life that tend to indicate how a couple will fare in the face of more extreme experiences. And, when there are major stressors, a couple's ability to navigate the day-to-day stressors can make difficult situations better or worse..

I am thinking about the different types of stressors people face as I sit with Neira and Jon. In their relationship, they carry many layers of stress. Some of their stressors are those of daily living—fighting traffic on the interstate, dealing with a random flea infestation, and having to call the roofing company when there is a leak.

However, Neira and Jon also carry the pain of multiple sudden and traumatic losses within the past year.

When I ask Neira and Jon how they recall their ability to navigate their losses, they soften and hold hands. "It's the hardest thing we've ever been through," Neira shares through falling tears and a runny nose. "It still is. But honestly, we were each other's rocks. I couldn't have asked for a better partner at that time."

As Neira cries, Jon holds her on the couch. He doesn't say much, just kisses the top of Neira's head and rubs her arms. "We weren't disagreeing so much on daily living things before the deaths. We were easygoing," Jon shares.

Because Jon and Neira could handle the daily, acute stressors and were getting along well, they had room within themselves to absorb the stress of loss and become closer rather than moving further apart. It did not change that the events were traumatic or painful, but it did create a capacity to be present with each other.

As they sit on my couch, it's not the death of loved ones that is pulling them apart. It's the compounding of daily stress. For Jon, external and internal stressors are tangling together, electrifying his nervous system and creating loops of anxiety. Neira, on the other hand, is so worried about her relationship with Jon—a stressor within their relationship—that she feels frozen and deactivated everywhere else in her life.

This dynamic has led them both into a pattern of being "activated" in different ways. Jon needs a solution-focused partner—one that will roll up their sleeves to help solve the problems—in order to feel grounded and soothed. But Neira needs an emotionally present partner before she can even begin looking at solutions.

As Neira and Jon look at their lists together, I ask them to take a deep breath and find a way to validate and recognize each person's stress.

"Even if the items on your partner's list don't stress you out, accept that these things stress out your partner. Also, don't give yourselves a hard time. We need to work on all this stress," I say, "but you need to start with compassion. Compassion means you can see someone is suffering and that you also feel motivated to help relieve that suffering with them. I need you to both agree to have some compassion here."

Jon and Neira soften. They hold each other's hands and agree. This is where we all need to start if we are going to change the impact of stress on the state of our relationships: identifying it, naming it, having a softness about the pain it causes, and having a determination to relieve the suffering.

SESSION NOTES:

In this session, we explored the different types of stress and how they appear in the body. We were focused on bringing "stress to life," or making it obvious that the stress under the surface actually exists. You can see this by tracking your BPM, getting in touch with your body and learning how to self-soothe, and making a list of all your stressors. You can also note whether you tend to become the cobra, the deer, or the opossum when you're stressed and how that impacts your relationship. Bringing stress to the surface might bring up difficult feelings about yourself or your partner, so we also focused on the importance of compassion. Use the interventions below to identify stress, soothe it, and accept yourself and your partner from a place of lovingkindness.

1. INTERVENTION: TRACK YOUR BPM

You don't have to come to my therapy office to track your stress states. You can monitor your own BPM at home using an Apple Watch or another similar device, or by buying your own pulse oximeter. Next time you are in conflict, take a look at the device. If your heart rate is above one hundred BPM (this number might be lower for people who are athletic or on heart medications), then it means you are in a stress state. Use this as a signal to begin self-soothing.

2. INTERVENTION: COBRAS, DEER, AND OPOSSUMS, OH MY!

Identify your go-to stress response. Are you the cobra who turns against their partner, the deer who runs away, or the opossum who shuts down and plays dead? All of these reactions are normal responses to stress, and you can begin to use the tools in this book to recognize and soothe yourself so you can become more cooperative with your partner.

3. INTERVENTION: SELF-SOOTHING

You can self-soothe by:

- **Taking deep breaths.** Breathe in through your nose, down through your belly, and slowly out of your mouth.

- **Moving around.** Ask your partner to give you a moment to walk to the kitchen and grab a drink.

- **Slowing down.** Try slowing down your voice and your movements.

- **Counting awareness.** Look outside and count the things you see or hear. How many plants do you see? How many houses? How many birds do you hear? This helps get you outside of your body and into the present moment.

By tracking your stress states, you can help your body feel safe and secure so that your relationships feel that way too.

4. INTERVENTION: IDENTIFYING STRESS (DARLA'S INTERVENTION)

Take a pad of paper and write down all of your stressors. A stressor is an experience or event that releases stress hormones. There are two types of stressors—physiological (your body) and psychological (your mind). You can use the examples below to help you begin to think through your own physical and psychological stressors. Set a timer for five minutes and write.

Examples of physical stressors:

- Cold or hot weather

- Bright lights

- Loud noises

- Chronic illness

- Pain

- Exhaustion

- Injury

- Too much substance use (caffeine, alcohol, drugs)

- Hunger

- Pregnancy

Examples of psychological stressors:

- Not being able to find a babysitter when you need to get to work

- Rudeness from other people

- Conflict with people

- Isolation and loneliness

- Financial concerns (paying taxes, not being up-to-date on bills)

- Work deadlines

- Changes in life (death of a loved one, losing a job, moving across the country, having a baby)

5. INTERVENTION: CREATE A BREAK RITUAL

Alongside your partner, come up with a break ritual. Just like Neira and Jon, you might become flooded from time to time. When people are flooded (overwhelmed) in a conversation, continuing to talk does not help. Instead, you'll need to take at least twenty minutes to allow the stress within your body to be reduced enough to reengage in conversation.

During a calm moment, agree with your partner on:

- How to initiate a break during a difficult conversation

- How to return to the conversation after the break

6. INTERVENTION: BE COMPASSIONATE

Work on noticing the pain and suffering of your partner and consider how you might help to relieve their suffering. It is common to react negatively to our partner's stress, but instead, we want to respond with lovingkindness. You can practice by asking your partner to share what was stressful about their day, and as you listen, practice keeping your body calm and present.

When you feel the need to correct them or solve their problems, instead offer them empathy and show curiosity.

CHAPTER 3

Soothe

O ther than a few streams of sunlight peeking through a crack in the curtains, it's dark in here. It's half past noon, but I've tried to make George's room a place where he can fall asleep. I walk from the door to his crib and touch my hand to his forehead. *He's still so hot*, I think. I touch his diaper. *It's still dry*.

My mind starts to race. George has been sick for over a week and it's not getting better. I knew something was wrong when he wouldn't stop crying. I took him to the doctor, who hypothesized it was an ear infection. She sent us home with some antibiotics and told us to come back in a week if it wasn't getting better. But two nights ago, he was up crying in the middle of the night and was clearly in extreme pain. I took his temperature and it was way too high, so I rushed him to the ER.

We were never seen, but by the time we decided to leave, his temperature had lowered. Now, he's in bed and just wants to sleep all day. He isn't really eating or peeing or crying.

I reach down and pick him up. He briefly looks at me and then closes his eyes again. *This isn't like him*. My heart is racing. I know something is wrong, but the doctors haven't seemed to think so. *I have to stay calm*, I remind myself. Otherwise, I won't be able to think through what to do.

I take a deep breath and exhale. I do that a few more times as I walk back and forth across the room.

I call Andrew and tell him to meet me at the ER—*a different one this time*.

We meet at a pediatric ER in a different town. George's fever is so high and he looks so lethargic that they take him back right away.

The nurse who takes his vitals is calm and measured. She smiles at us and reassures us that he is in good hands. I find myself feeling calmer in her presence. Once she leaves the room, it's just Andrew and me watching George lay on the hospital cot.

Suddenly, his eyes roll back in his head and he goes limp.

"George!" Andrew screams. He rushes to the bed and grabs and shakes him. Andrew's face is panicked and I am frozen. "George, wake up, please wake up." Everything is in slow motion. The noisy hospital goes silent in my mind because all I can hear is the ringing in my ears. I want to say something, but nothing comes out. Suddenly, things speed up. I run out to the hallway and scream, "Help! Help! Please."

A nurse rushes in, and just as she does, his eyes flutter open. He's okay.

My body is shaking and Andrew is white as a ghost. The nurse grabs my hand. "He's okay, mama. But let me get the doctor in here right now so we make sure that doesn't happen again."

I walk over to Andrew and hug him. He hugs me back. We both cry as we stroke each other's backs. I feel my muscles relax and my heart calm. I can take a deep breath.

YOU'RE SAFE

Society often focuses on self-regulation, which is the ability to manage thoughts and feelings in a way that allows you to still function within your values and maintain your relationships. However, co-regulation is the first step on the path toward learning self-regulation.

When I was in the hospital, the doctors, nurses, and Andrew helped to soothe me. When they smiled or offered words of reassurance, my heart rate would lower and some of my focus would return. When Andrew would hug me or squeeze my hand, I could come back into the moment even if I had been taken so very far away because of my distress.

Research shows that the people around us, especially romantic partners, play a role in our physiological stress responses. One study showed that if someone is in pain and they hold their romantic partner's hand, their pain is reduced. Another study showed that if one partner is stressed and has raised levels of cortisol, their partner will mirror this stressed state. This means the alternative would also be true—that when one partner is calm and relaxed, it helps the other to feel the same way too.[2]

These outcomes are due to a process called co-regulation. This is the process of a person with a regulated nervous system being able to share their calm state with someone who has a dysregulated nervous system. Essentially, it is the act of sharing your calm. You might do this through having a calm voice, remaining patient, or showing affection.

Imagine a parent with a baby. Cross-culturally, as a baby cries, a parent tends to naturally respond with specific actions—they sway, hold the baby closer, lower their voice, and hum. While all of these things tend to soothe a baby because they mimic the womb experience, they also help to soothe and regulate the parent. The humming and swaying soothes the parent, which in turn can assist the baby in their process of self-soothing. Calm bodies can calm other bodies.

While human beings are wired to love, they are also wired to be combative. We are constantly in a battle with our nervous system in regard to deciding if an upsetting moment is a time to cooperate or be combative. It's important in safe, loving relationships to work hard to build that muscle to behave with love as often as possible by offering warmth and responsiveness, even in difficult moments.

Couple Profile

Haseem (32/M) and Sarita (28/F) have been in couples therapy for about a month. Haseem is a police officer and Sarita works as a real estate agent. They have been together for ten years. They find themselves arguing a lot recently and are worried about their future. Haseem and Sarita come to therapy hoping to learn conflict management skills and to get on the same page.

I'm trudging up the stairs in my home with a coffee in hand. It's half past two in the afternoon, but I am still wearing my pajama pants. I had a few minutes to put on a bra and a professional top. My hair is combed back so you can't tell, at least on video, that I haven't had a shower today.

I open my laptop, sign into SimplePractice, and click "start" on the telehealth appointment I'm about to have. As the video opens, I see Haseem and Sarita sitting very close together, but it's only so they are both in the frame. I can tell that they wish they were sitting far from one another.

"Hi, Haseem. Hi, Sarita. I can tell something is up, so why don't we just dive in?"

Haseem looks at Sarita as if he is asking her whether he should go first. She rolls her eyes and says, "If you aren't going to start, I will. Let's not waste time here."

Sarita adjusts her head covering before continuing. "Quite frankly, Liz, I am really angry right now. We got a tax bill in the mail today, and I am just shocked. I was under the impression Haseem was taking care of it." She crosses her arms over her chest. Haseem tries to make eye contact with her, but she turns her face away, looking at the opposite wall.

I know Haseem is looking to her to regulate himself. He's hoping to see a brief smile or to see her body turn toward his so he can know that they are on the same page. He doesn't see it though, and in the split second it takes to process that, he becomes activated.

He smirks. *Ugh, great, they are both dysregulating each other*, I think. He then lets out a sarcastic, snort-like laugh. "Yeah, I knew this was a waste of time today. You know what, Liz, I'm not going to do this. Thanks for everything but I'm done . . ."

He starts waving his hands around, indicating he's about to close the computer and shut down the session. I take a deep inhale. I can hear that his mouth is dry and his eyes look wide, as if caught by surprise.

As I see them escalate each other, I start to notice frustration in my own body as I feel their distress. I rub the leg of my soft pajama pants to bring myself back to the present moment, and then I inhale and exhale.

"Haseem. Wait just a moment." I continue to breathe. I continue to ground my body and lower my voice. I slow down my cadence and say, "You're both very stressed right now. Let's take a breath together." Then I audibly inhale and let out a sigh. I see Haseem start to calm down slightly. So my eyes move to Sarita.

She has turned her body toward Haseem. Her eyebrow is raised and her lip is pulled back. She is angry. "*Real mature*, Haseem. You make a mistake and you don't want to talk about," she says.

The cycle is going to continue—Haseem will feel Sarita's distress and dysregulate and then Sarita will feel Haseem's dysregulation and dysregulate more. If they weren't in a therapy session, this would continue on and on until someone stomped out of the room.

"Okay, both of you, I need you to pause. Take a deep breath."

I slow it down a little. Taking a longer pause before speaking again and making sure my voice is measured and calm. As things slow down, I can see both of them coming to a more regulated space. I don't have to direct them to do anything, and yet I can see they've started to calm down because I've started to calm down.

"You both look calmer—how are you feeling?"

"I feel better," Sarita says as Haseem nods his head in agreement. "Okay, good. So, look, something really stressful happened today. I can see that. It happened and it is scary—tax bills are always scary—but you're dysregulating each other with this issue rather than soothing each other, coming together, and problem-solving."

I take a pause for a sip of water and gesture for them to take a sip of theirs too, then I continue.

"When people are upset in the presence of another person, there are two directions it can go—either the people will dysregulate each other and make it worse, or they will act in ways that promote self-regulation and will act as a cue to the other person, tell them that they are safe."

I go on to explain that while it might feel good in the moment to yell at your partner, or scoff at them, or blame them, all it does is increase stress. I teach them about how the body responds to stress and how behaving in this way will only make things worse. I remind them that people can only be relational when they feel safe.

"I want you to work together to help each other feel safe when upsetting situations arise in your marriage. Otherwise you won't be allies; you'll be enemies."

Sarita leans toward Haseem. I can't see below the screen, but based on the relief in his face, I believe she's grabbed his hand.

SELF-REGULATION

Because it's hard to do relational activities like play, problem solve, be curious, and be affectionate when you're physiologically flooded, you'll have to first respond to what is happening within your body in order to change the way stress impacts your relationship. **Learning self-regulation skills will help you to do this.**

Co-regulation can occur when at least one person in the relationship is able to utilize self-regulation skills. I always tell my couples that it truly only takes one person to change the trajectory. If you can learn to self-regulate, you'll be able to get yourself to a calmer state and share that state with those around you when needed.

Self-regulation might be a process that can happen quickly or it might take time. For example, when I am in session and I start to feel upset, I regulate myself within moments by taking deep breaths, refocusing, or using mindfulness to ground myself. However, when my husband and I are in conflict, I might need to self-regulate by taking a walk or spending some time in my room, alone, with a book.

Self-regulation is the ability to control your behavior, emotions, and thoughts in the pursuit of long-term goals. For the sake of this book, the long-term goal is to feel better with yourself and to feel better with your partner.

It requires an observance of feelings (physical and emotional) and the ability to remember that pain is temporary. Something significant changes when you can "make friends" with your pain. When you get to know it, understand it, and pay attention to what it needs in order to pass through you.

Overall, being present with your discomfort is an important aspect of self-regulation. According to research, "The ability to control behavior enables humans to live cooperatively, achieve important goals, and maintain health throughout the life span."[3] Controlling your behavior requires self-regulation. This is a difficult task for many. Whether it's because your nervous system has been impacted by trauma, because you've been trained to react poorly in certain situations, or because of the millions of temptations we all face day in and day out, people often react instinctively and impulsively rather than responding constructively.

When people experience stress, it becomes even more difficult to self-regulate. Uncomfortable emotions are the most common cause of what is called self-regulation failure. This makes sense on two levels:

- When we feel uncomfortable, it's human nature to do anything to quickly remove the discomfort (even if it won't help in the long run).

- Stress inherently makes us more irritable, less curious, and worse problem solvers. This takes away our ability to think clearly and choose from alternative options.

And yet, even those who struggle with self-regulation the most can learn how to put self-regulation into practice and develop the muscle. With more self-regulation, you become more in control of your life and better able to make decisions from a conscious space rather than from an emotional space. In building self-regulation your ultimate goal is to learn how to pause between an emotional sensation and your reaction to it.

This ability is commonly known in dialectical behavior therapy as the "wise mind." The wisest mind we can create is one that combines our thinking *and our feelings*.

When I meet with couples, I can tell that they are living with their emotional mind if they are continually doing things that feel good in the moment but create long-term harm. Examples include:

- Saying hurtful things to their partner that they don't really mean, but that come out explosively due to frustration.

- Spending money, time, or energy that they don't really have in response to unrecognized feeling impulses. For example, planning a trip they can't afford because life feels so stressful, having a second child because they feel lonely and disconnected from each other, or signing their kid up for another after-school activity because they feel guilty about some sort of perceived lack when it comes to parenting.

- Partaking in avoidance activities that hurt their relationship, things like drinking or working too much or spending so much time with other people that the relationship unit suffers.

- Withdrawing into oneself in response to emotional discomfort by playing constant video games, checking emails all of the time, or sitting on their phone.

I can also tell that they've leaned too far into their rational thinking mind if they are:

- No longer taking risks together.

- Stressing about the things they believe they can control by over planning and over-researching.

- Working too hard to explain everything from their brain space without listening enough to their heart space. They might say things to each other like, "What you're feeling doesn't even make sense . . ." followed by rational reasons as to why it doesn't.

When couples can learn to combine their emotional mind with their rational mind, they become wise together. They have the capacity to be emotion coaches *and solution coaches. Wise minds create aha moments and help people become unstuck.*

Wise mind occurs when you can step back from the situation and observe the way you are thinking and feeling. Wise mind in a relationship means being able to observe yourself and be curious with your partner. When we can self-regulate, we allow ourselves to step back and take in the big picture. And part of that picture becomes seeing the other person.

A few months later, Sarita and Haseem come back to see me. They've been able to work out the issue with the tax bill together. It turned out it was a clerical error at the IRS. They aren't in therapy because they are arguing; they are here because Sarita has been having flashbacks to a traumatic experience in her childhood and has also just left her job. She and Haseem noticed she was highly distressed.

During the session, Sarita begins to share a vivid story of childhood abuse and she is in distress. Instead of shutting down, Haseem sees her pain and takes a deep breath in and a deep breath out. He focuses on lowering his heart rate as she speaks, and he lowers his voice. He shares his calm. Sarita feels that Haseem is safe and calm in his own body, and rather than go into fight mode, Sarita feels safe enough to soften into sadness. This time, under the screen, I see Haseem reach his hand toward her lap. Then, he wraps his other arm around her and rocks back and forth.

LETTING OUR STRESS CYCLE COMPLETE

When we are being chased by a lion, our stress cycle completes through the exertion we put forth to keep ourselves safe, and then, once we arrive to safety, the signals we receive that we are safe. Unfortunately, many of our modern-day stressors don't allow us to complete our stress cycle in this way. This isn't to say our stress responses aren't due to something serious, but usually they aren't related to a life-or-death situation, so the cycle doesn't play out. When this doesn't happen, it puts our relational and physical well-being at risk.

The stress cycle ends when you do the things only a safe person can do. The most common examples are slow breaths, moving your body in a playful way (exercise, dance, or stretching), sleeping, and spending time with people you love. After a particularly overwhelming event, I encourage you to do one of these things.

While the rest of this book will focus on important decisions you'll need to make and coping skills you'll need to build in order to live a stress-reduced lifestyle, self-regulation and co-regulation are the foundation. If you continue to work on these, you'll be on the path toward reducing stress—and its impacts—on your relationship.

SESSION NOTES:

In this session, we learned about co-regulation. Co-regulation is the ability to calm your own body, calm your partner's body, and avoid entering into a co-escalatory experience. By practicing the interventions below, you'll be able to calm your body and, in turn, calm your partner's body so you can both come back to the present moment and connect.

1. INTERVENTION: CO-REGULATION

You can calm yourself and your partner by trying the following:

- Speak with a slow, soft voice
- Wear a gentle facial expression—check the tension in your jaw and allow your mouth to drop open a bit; pay attention to your brow and avoid furrowing
- Drop your shoulders
- Inhale into your belly, hold, and slowly exhale

2. INTERVENTION: BOX BREATHING

When you're experiencing high levels of stress, individually or relationally, box breathing can remind your body that it is safe. Breathing is our body's natural relaxation system. Imagine a box. Starting on the left side of the box inhale for four seconds, tracing the line upwards, then move to the top of the box, holding the air in your belly for four seconds. Then move to the right side of the box and slowly exhale for four seconds before moving to the bottom of the box and holding the air in your belly for another four seconds. Repeat until your body feels calm.

3. INTERVENTION: WISE MIND

Our wisest mind combines our thinking and our feelings. When we are physiologically flooded, it's difficult to combine the two. In order to cope, we either lean into our emotional mind or our rational mind. This creates a scenario where we leave out important information. In relationships, this leads to unfair assessments and arguments.

Wise mind requires the use of the word *and*—being able to ask yourself to connect the rational and the emotional will help you to use your wise mind in conflict. For example, "I am feeling so angry right now and I know that I tend to calm down the next day," or "Of course I see a rational solution to the entire issue and I can also allow myself to see how frustrating this feels."

CHAPTER 4

Have Intimacy

t's been six weeks since George was born, and I'm sitting in the waiting room of my OB-GYN. I look down at George, who is snoozing in his car seat, and continue to rock him back and forth using my foot. Trekking to the city was difficult. George kept crying in the back seat and I hit traffic at every turn. Now, I've been waiting for forty-five minutes and he's getting fussy. I'm not sure how much longer he or I can wait.

Finally I hear "Elizabeth" called from the swinging door at the front of the room. I pick up George's car seat and follow a nurse, who takes my vitals and drops me in an exam room. The doctor arrives and checks out the results of my C-section and does an internal exam.

I'm wondering how it's possible that this is the extent of the first follow-up appointment after birth. Is she going to check in on me and discover how much I'm struggling emotionally?

She doesn't. But what she does say is that I am cleared for sex and exercise. *Woohoo*, I think sarcastically, *the last two things I want to do!*

I leave the office and text my husband the good news. I'm trying to be sexy and fun with some emoji innuendo, but I'm not feeling it. My breasts are leaking, George is screaming, and I feel uncomfortable in my body. According to the text I get back, my husband is definitely feeling it.

I get home and think the rest of the day about how much I want to feel sexually close to my husband, while also wondering if it's going to "have to" happen tonight. When the sun goes down and we get into bed, he makes a move. I let him know I'm tired.

"Oh, okay babe," he says and gives me a kiss. I turn over. I hear him turn over too and let out a big sigh. The light from his phone reflects off the opposite wall. I know he's upset.

I lay awake thinking about how I am failing him. About how strange it is to go from a relationship where you stay actively engaged in bed all day to one where all you want to do is roll over and fall asleep.

As time goes on, I learn it's not that I am failing him. It's that, for me, stress puts a hard brake on any sex drive I have during the best of times.

This, though, is no consolation to my husband, who feels as if I don't love him anymore. He internalizes my distance and it begins to impact his self-esteem. Our lack of sex due to my stressors becomes a stressor for him. Our conversations about it become awkward and hurtful.

"It's because of my stress," I try and explain.

"That doesn't make sense," he responds. "Sex is supposed to help people feel better about their stress."

I take a deep inhale. I am frustrated. *Why would I make this up?* I think. I try to explain to him that everyone is different—while some seek out sexual activity to reduce stress, other people avoid it.

Several months later, I am doing some consulting work with a relationship health company. They are offering a workshop on sex that they want me to to attend. Self-help isn't Andrew's thing, but supporting me is, so we go. In the workshop, the presenter explains that for some people, stress is a deterrent to sex, and for others it relieves it. Andrew looks over at me and jokingly offers, "See, I told you so." I smile. I am relieved he can take this in. And I remind myself to also take in the reality that not everyone shuts down sexually during stress.

The presenter goes on to share the concept of accelerators and brakes from Emily Nagoski, a sex educator and researcher.[1] Accelerators are the things that turn you on and get you ready for the hot stuff, while brakes make you less likely to feel open to engaging. The presenter shares that accelerators can include anything from sexy lingerie to a clean house or a day off from work, while brakes can include too many dishes in the sink, a bad smell, or the thought of losing your job.

This concept is greatly helpful to Andrew and me. It legitimizes that we are different people with different needs, and it also provides a road map for how to create environments and experiences that include more accelerators than brakes. We become a team on this—our job, together, is to remove each other's brakes not just for sexy time, but for a peaceful life overall. It also becomes each of our responsibilities to create an environment that is primed for intimacy so we can both take part in pressing on the accelerator.

SEX AND STRESS

In my thousands of hours of work with couples, I know that Andrew and I aren't alone in our sexual and intimacy challenges in the face of stress. Sex, like other forms of closeness, is negatively impacted when people are stressed for long periods of time. Unfortunately, I have also found that many couples don't pinpoint their lack of a sex life to stress; they instead resort to blaming themselves or the other person. They tell themselves stories like, "My partner must not love me anymore," or "I'm just not sexy enough." And, as they tell themselves these stories, their relationship with sex and each other becomes more complicated and difficult to touch. The already taboo topic becomes more fraught with anxiety and pain, grows legs, and becomes a monster.

When sex isn't going well for one or both members of a couple, some common beliefs that arise are:

- If my partner loved me, then we would have a great sex life.

- If they cared about how I felt, they would prioritize sex.

- If we can't get our sex life together, perhaps we should get a divorce.

- My partner doesn't have a sex drive now and probably won't have one again.

- I understand my partner is stressed, but if they really desired me, we would still be having sex.

Not only is a couple's ability to navigate conflict impacted by stress, but so is their sex life. This is because of psychological reasons—stress is distracting—but also because of changes in hormones, like an increase in cortisol, which is related to stress. Research has shown that physiologically, stress is negatively correlated with sexual behavior and satisfaction between couples. For women, high levels of chronic stress are related to the loss of many aspects of sexual pleasure—including lower levels of genital sexual arousal. For men, stress impacts erectile function.[2]

Like anything else relating to stress, it's important to think about how to navigate sex as a team. When couples work toward coping with stress and facing the side effects of it together, they improve their outcome. One step is depersonalizing the issue (even though, I know, it's deeply personal) and working toward understanding the physiological impacts of stress on sex. When you do this, you can work together to remove barriers to sexy time.

Couple Profile

Tiffany (40/F) and Chris (35/M) have been together for six years. They are married and have two children. Tiffany works as a bus driver and Chris worked in construction—however, he recently lost his job. Tiffany and Chris come to therapy to navigate conflict around their sexual relationship.

I'm sitting in a bedroom at my dad's beach condo. Andrew told me he would hold down the fort with family while I took a few days away from the house to focus on work. My dad's condo was available, so I drove down for a few quiet winter days at the shore. It's been nice to wake up, get a coffee, and not have to worry about anything but myself for the day. I feel grateful to my husband, who recognizes when I need a break.

I'm fiddling around behind the bed, looking for the outlet. I need to plug in my computer for a session I have in a few minutes. Chris and Tiffany have been seeing me for a few months now. They first came in because they recognized that something significant was happening to their relationship, and they didn't know how to fix it. They described endless nights laying in the same bed with their backs to each other. "Going to bed feels painful now," Tiffany shared. "I know as soon as I lay down, we are both going to ignore the elephant in the room. It's just awkward."

Tiffany said that she wants to be close to Chris but finds that when she reaches out to cuddle him or leans over to offer a kiss, it is like trying to connect with a brick wall. "I get nothing in return," she said. "He kind of accepts the touch but doesn't reciprocate."

Chris becomes defensive in our sessions. He asks her things like, "What do you expect from me when I feel like shit about myself?" Or, "Don't you see I am tired at the end of the night?" Chris lost his job five months ago and hasn't been able to find steady work since. He's found himself in a crisis of identity—a man who identifies as a masculine provider for his family is now home watching the news most days. He hasn't been able to contribute to their bills. To him, none of this is acceptable. And he can't understand how it is possible that Tiffany finds him desirable.

Tiffany doesn't understand why Chris doesn't believe her when she says she is still into him. Instead, she tells herself a convoluted story to make sense of it. "I think he uses this all as a justification for just not being into me," she shared. This belief makes Tiffany feel rejected, shut down, and unsure of whether or not she is wanted and desired in the relationship.

I finally find the outlet and my laptop makes the "ding" sound to let me know it's getting the electricity it needs. I pull the screen open and click "start" on the virtual appointment. Tiffany and Chris sit across from me, many miles away. They look tired and upset. "Good morning!" I say. "I can tell something is going on, so let's jump right in."

Before I can say more, Tiffany starts to cry. "I don't think things can get better, Liz. It's so obvious that Chris doesn't love me anymore, and I can't take it. I left the house last night because it was just too upsetting to lay in bed beside someone who doesn't even want me to be there."

Tiffany is like the fleeing deer, who runs when distressed. She takes a big inhale as she continues to cry. She is defeated and feels rejected.

I look toward Chris who is looking somewhere off-screen. I don't see a man who doesn't love his wife; I see a man who feels ashamed that right now he can't love her in the way he believes he should. He is stressed and defeated. "Chris," I say gently. "What are you thinking?"

"I don't know what else to say," he says quietly. "I am failing her everywhere. Especially if she doesn't believe I love her. I already know I'm not enough . . . but hearing it again and again is too much for me."

I take a deep breath. I know that so much of this has been created by an internal dialogue they both have about what it means to have desire and be desirable. So much of it isn't informed by what their partner is saying, but by what they believe in their mind to be true.

"I think you are both telling yourselves stories that aren't true instead of listening to what is actually happening."

They look at me. "What do you mean?" Tiffany asks. "Of course it's true. In happy relationships people have sex. When people are into each other, they have sex. This isn't some made-up story. It's reality."

"Yeah, and it's also a reality that there is no way in hell a woman could be attracted to a man who isn't working," says Chris.

"I am sorry to tell you that neither of those things are actually reality. They are things you think, but they aren't the only truth. You aren't listening to each other," I continue. "You are letting the stories you tell yourself be louder than what your partner is sharing."

I ask them to both repeat their stance. Tiffany shares with Chris that she is attracted to him, that she does desire him, and that the job situation doesn't impact that at all for her. I ask Chris to take it in. Chris shares with Tiffany that his lack of desire and sexual energy is related to feeling incredible stress and disappointment in himself. I ask Tiffany to take that in too.

I go on to share with them that stress impacts libido—the desire you have for sex. That it isn't always true that a lack of "drive" is due to disinterest or lack of love. For Tiffany and Chris, there is no easy fix to the stress Chris is feeling. Tiffany will need to be patient as he finds his way and understand that right now he doesn't feel like himself and is stressed about work and finances, but will ultimately be okay.

The lull in sex isn't the issue—but it will become an issue if they feel stressed about the stress, adding so many layers that a molehill becomes a mountain.

I ask Chris to talk about his brakes. He has a lot right now. When he notices the bills are racking up, when he sees Tiffany leave for work as he sits on the couch, and whenever he gets another job rejection email. All of these things slow down his energy for sex. "Right now, even the things that used to be accelerators are brakes," he shares. "The other night Tiffany put on sexy lingerie, and all I thought was, 'I don't deserve this.'"

I work with Tiffany to understand that every long-term relationship has sexual lulls. I encourage Chris to reassure Tiffany that he loves her, is attracted to her, and is hopeful for a day when their sex life returns to "normal." Tiffany begins to hear the challenges Chris was feeling from a place of empathy rather than from a place of fear. I encourage her to let him talk about his stress without rushing to make it better for him. When Tiffany learns that this is all she has to do for the moment, she feels relief. When Chris hears he wasn't failing her, some of his confidence returns.

As Tiffany and Chris get better at accepting the lull in their sex lives and talking about how they both experience stress, we begin to talk about how to increase the "accelerators" that create an environment conducive to intimacy for both of them. Chris shares that even when he is down on himself, he feels the energy to have sex after having a good experience with Tiffany. Tiffany shares that while she is almost always open to having sex, she feels especially close and connected to Chris when they spend time being affectionate during the day.

Over the next several months, Chris works on coming to terms with his own narratives about gender, finding activities that helped him feel purposeful, and eventually gained employment. Tiffany waited patiently from a place of empathy and love as they lived through the season together.

HOW STRESS AFFECTS LIBIDO

The hormones that are released when you feel stress provide a quick shot of energy that helps you handle a threat in the moment—allowing you to fight it or run away from it. If the stress can be dealt with, the response subsides and your body gets a signal that it's okay now. This signal allows you to go back to baseline.

However, if stress is being experienced over a long period of time, the body never gets the signal that everything is okay. If this continues, the body will continue to produce more and more cortisol. This process, over time, reduces testosterone production in men and women, which is highly important to your sex drive.[3] So, if you've noticed that you're just not into sex, ask yourself if you've been stressed for a long period of time. Have there been chronic work stressors? Major parenting transitions? Health issues? Financial worries?

If your partner has been telling you that their lack of desire has to do with their stress, you can now believe that it's true. There really is a physiological process that happens within the body in response to overwhelming situations. And it impacts sex drive.

Beyond the change in hormones, couples struggling with their sex life are also impacted by the ways in which they think and relate to each other when stressed. As we discussed, it becomes harder to listen, be curious, and problem solve when someone is under a constant bombardment of worry.

Just like it's hard to talk about a vacation when a lion wants to eat you, it can also be difficult to enjoy kissing, to give yourself permission to lay around and cuddle, or to fantasize about erotic experiences. Our minds don't like to think about the things we do when we are safe when we feel like we are in danger.

Stressed people also tend to want more time alone, and they might begin to see their partner's attempts to connect intimately as a violation of their space and react by withdrawing further or becoming aggressive and irritable. The stressed person feels more and more disrespected over time. For example, when my husband would sigh after I said I wasn't in the mood, I started to think, *Why would you even try when you know what kind of day I've had!* Meanwhile, the other person begins to feel rejected and alone.

INTIMACY ISN'T JUST SEX

We often use the word *intimacy* as code for sex. But intimacy is about a special kind of closeness you feel with another person—and there are many ways to feel it. If your sex life is hurting, you might want to consider other types of intimacy. When Chris shared with Tiffany that doing activities together helps him feel more confident and connected, Tiffany was able to successfully find ways to be close to him. They worked together to plan hikes and started going fishing on Saturdays.

Doing this improved the relationship in a few ways. It helped Tiffany to feel seen and cared about by Chris due to the quality time he offered her, and it helped Chris feel good about life and himself. It filled up their emotional bank account—giving them more opportunity for good moments together.

All of this acts as a stress reducer in the relationship, which can also improve the sexual relationship.

Couples can experience intimacy with each other emotionally, intellectually, experientially, spiritually, physically, and sexually. Emotional intimacy is when we believe we can share our feelings with each other in a safe way. Intellectual intimacy is the closeness we feel when we learn something together or talk about something interesting. Experiential intimacy happens when we do exciting or novel activities together. Spiritual intimacy occurs when you feel awe together. And physical intimacy includes hand holding, touching, and cuddling.

Expanding the ways in which you feel close reduces stress and increases closeness and a reassuring sense that you matter to each other.

TALKING ABOUT IT

Sex is one of the most difficult topics for couples to approach. Because of this, partners often enter the conversation with a lot of trepidation. They tend to be unclear with each other and fill in the knowledge gaps with their own stories. These stories only make things worse.

When couples rip the Band-Aid off and talk about stress and sex (or any other avoided topic), their relationship improves. Couples can have what is called a dyadic coping conversation to be present and aware of each other's stress—using empathy, understanding, and curiosity to help their partner cope with their internal stress. They can also spend time talking about what they think about sex, what they desire, and what they hope for. However, they must learn to do this without becoming reactive to each other or shaming each other's beliefs.

Beyond talking, couples can use safety-promoting behaviors with each other, like play and gentle touch, to reduce the stress response in each other's bodies, opening the door to the possibility for sexual connection.

SESSION NOTES:

In this session, we explored how sex drive is impacted by stress. The interventions below will help you address how stress is impacting your sex life from a place of love. Learning to accept that physiology can have an impact, that our sex lives experience lulls, that everyone has different accelerators and brakes that fluctuate from time to time, and that there are other ways to connect, can help to reduce the likelihood that your sex life becomes just another stressor.

1. INTERVENTION: IDENTIFYING YOUR ACCELERATORS AND BRAKES

Talk with each other about your "turn-ons" and "turn-offs." Share with your partner the contexts, environments, and sensations that tend to put the pedal to the metal and what tends to slam on the brakes.
Examples of accelerators include:

Contexts

- Feeling good at work

- Feeling proud of your parenting

- Being away from home

- Following exercise

Environments

- A clean house

- The bedroom

- Somewhere new and novel

Sensations

- Good smells

- Light touch

- A dark room with a lit candle

Examples of brakes include:

Contexts

- Feeling insecure at work

- Getting bad news about your health

- Feeling like you need to shower

Environments

- A messy house

- Away from home

Sensations

- Bad smells

- Painful touch

- Loud sounds

2. INTERVENTION: TALK ABOUT IT

Talk about stress with your partner by asking open-ended, empathetic questions and by listening. For example, you can ask questions like:

"What has been the most stressful part of this experience for you?"

"What do you need to feel better?"

These questions give your partner permission to discuss their stress without you jumping in to fix it or disagree with it.

Talk about sex by asking curious and open questions like:

"How are you feeling about our sex life lately?"

"What puts you in the mood?"

"What turns you off?"

3. INTERVENTION: FILL THE EMOTIONAL BANK ACCOUNT

Fill your emotional bank account by focusing on other areas of intimacy. Look at each category below and pay attention to how you and your partner fill your intimacy cups over the next week. Then, pick an area of intimacy to focus on together.

- Experiential Intimacy
- Intellectual Intimacy
- Physical Intimacy
- Sexual Intimacy
- Emotional Intimacy
- Spiritual Intimacy

CHAPTER 5

Stop Overpouring Your Cup

'm sitting on the deep windowsill of a bar on a cozy side street in Philadelphia's bustling Rittenhouse Square. I haven't been here since before I got married, and it reminds me of less stressful times when I was still young and had fewer obligations. I imagine myself back then feeling free with so much excitement and hope for the wonder of life that lay ahead. I turn my head away from people watching out the window and toward my husband, who sits at the table beside me. "I have an idea," I say.

I am feeling energized. We've finally gotten childcare worked out and I really think we are coming together on the whole mental load thing. Andrew has been coming home at more regular times and seems to be noticing more around the house—things like burnt-out lightbulbs and beeping fire alarms. And now, we are on a date. The type of date that actually feels fun.

"What's the idea?" He smiles.

"You're going to think I am crazy, but we've saved a little bit of money and I think we should buy a beach condo in the building where my dad has his."

"No way," Andrew retorts. But I know Andrew. I know his initial response is often an invitation to be convinced.

"Listen, I know the units are small and we don't have a lot of money, but I am just thinking we could use a project. And we could turn it into an Airbnb and make a little more money . . . that way if I ever want to spend more time at home, we have something subsidizing us."

He's quiet for a moment as he stares out the window at the people walking by. "You know," he says, "I would be open to it."

My heart flutters. I am excited to have a project that isn't related to being a mom or my job. Don't get me wrong, I love both, but sometimes it's nice to have something else too.

We spend the night crunching numbers over dinner and looking up listings. We impulsively email a realtor living in the beach town. Within a week, we are trekking to the beach to look at properties. The last property we see is the unit right next to my dad's. "It has good vibes," Andrew says. I agree.

We contact a lender who likely thinks we are crazy. We have exactly the amount needed for the down payment in our savings account. Somehow, he approves us anyway. Several weeks later, we are collecting keys, sprucing up the joint, and listing it on Airbnb.

And it's all fine. More than fine. This stress brings us closer together, helps us have a shared goal, and makes us feel like we are more than the strange version of ourselves we have been as of late.

Before buying our condo, our stress cup has room for more. So, we add to it. And over the next few years we will continue to add more and more and more.

Couple Profile

Tyler (42/M) and Ashley (35/F) have been married for eleven years and they have three children. Tyler works in New York City as an attorney and Ashley is an accountant. Tyler and Ashley present to therapy reporting that they no longer have a sex life and frequently fight on the weekends. They also admit that they are worried about how much they drink and how it impacts their relationship. They come to therapy to reignite their connection.

"This cup represents the two of you and the stress you carry," I say to Tyler and Ashley. I'm holding a full plastic cup of water in my hand to help them visualize a common metaphor I use. It's late on a Tuesday night and it's my last session of the evening. I've had a busy day, but Ashley and Tyler are new and I have looked forward to seeing them since our first session.

My dark office is mostly lit by the city lights outside my large nineteenth-story window and a tiny couch-side lamp. Ashley, a tall, slender woman, sits on my couch perfectly coiffed even though it's late in the evening. Her hands are tightly folded on her lap, her knees are clasped together, and her back is perfectly straight. This is a posture I call "the pin." It's the type of body language that exudes wanting to be seen as perfect but not really feeling that way inside. It's like the body is saying, *If I stay very still, maybe you won't see me.*

Tyler, the husband, sits next to her, their knees nearly touching. He is also smartly dressed, still in his suit and tie from a long day at the office. But, his knees fall apart from each other, his hands dangle between them, and his body curls forward, almost as if his head is ready to swan dive between his legs straight into the floor. This posture often indicates shame.

Neither Ashley nor Tyler feels good enough; it's clear just from looking at them. And yet, so much of their life is spent proving to themselves and others that they are more than good enough—that they are extraordinary.

"We love to be busy," Ashley shared in the first session.

"We've always been go-getters. Couldn't really imagine living any differently. It wouldn't be a full life," added Tyler.

But their life wasn't just full, it was overfilled. For them, living life to the fullest meant a never-ending list of projects, debts, activities, and illnesses. Like someone balancing plates at a circus, they were managing, but it was precarious.

Tyler, who had been working from home the past year, had to start going back to the office five days a week—which was two hours away in New York City. The plates started falling. Frequent fighting and less sex than ever before brought Ashley and Tyler to my couch asking, "Why aren't we connecting?" and "Why are we so on edge?"

So, on that late Tuesday night, I tried to help them answer those questions. I point to the cup of water in my hand and say, "You were carrying all of this stress before Tyler started commuting again. You were already at the brim, and you were lucky it wasn't overflowing."

I pause a moment to let them think while I grab another plastic cup of water.

"But then, Tyler had to start commuting again," I say, as I start to pour the second cup of water into the first. A smooth flow of water runs down the sides of the cup and onto the floor.

I continue, "He had to leave earlier in the morning and get home later. You had to add the cost of transportation into the mix, and only one of you is home to take care of the kids before and after school." The water keeps spilling out of the cup.

"That might have all been manageable," I say gently, "but then you made the decision to send the kids to a private school far away from your home. It's thirty minutes away without traffic. So now, Ashley commutes over two hours a day to get the kids to and from school."

Water keeps flowing.

"And then, something happened that was out of your control. Ashley's mom got sick. And so, Ashley has been having to help her mom manage her medical care."

More water.

"As if that wasn't enough, you decided to redo the bathrooms in your home. That's become a bigger project than you expected."

As water continues running onto the floor, I finally set the cup to the side.

"You're doing too much," I share. "Just too much. And it's impacting your relationship."

THE GOOD STRESS THAT'S NOT SO GOOD

It is 11:00 pm, and my parents are in the kitchen arguing again. I'm sitting in my blush pink room on my blush pink carpet with my knees up by my chest. I turned the light back on after my mom kissed me good night and have been writing in my journal and reading books, which is the only reason I am up to hear them. I can feel discomfort in my stomach as their mumbles become shouts, but it's not enough to interrupt what I am doing—I am focused.

But then, I hear banging in the kitchen and whatever is happening is starting to sound scary. My mom is crying and my dad is yelling. I slowly close my journal and pause for a moment to think about what to do next. I quietly step out of bed, open my door, and look down the hallway. It's dark and quiet but I am worried about my sisters. In my long pink nightgown, I quietly shuffle to the opposite end of the hallway where my middle sister sleeps. I open her door and peek into the room. It's dark and she doesn't seem to be moving. She's not awake.

Next, I walk toward my youngest sister's room. She is about three or four and has the sweetest brunette bowl cut, big brown eyes, and a beauty mark above her lip. She's particularly sensitive—more so than my middle sister—and I feel the need to protect her.

I lean my ear against her door, trying to hear if there is noise inside. I don't want to wake her up if she is asleep, but I also don't want to leave her alone if she is awake and scared. I slowly open the door and see her lying in bed with her eyes wide open staring at the ceiling.

"Hey sweetie," I whisper. "Why are you up?"

"Yelling," she says.

I walk into her room and pull back her white, shabby-chic bed cover. She has a My Little Pony nightgown on and cute bare feet. She is precious and upset. "It's ok," I say, as I wrap my arm around her, pull the cover up, and cuddle her back to sleep.

As the years go on, I continue to use hyper-focus and caretaking to manage my own feelings. It's not a bad combination—being productive and loving. I rearrange my room frequently, start entrepreneurial projects like pen pal clubs and lemonade stands, and think up stories, write them out, crumble them up, and start again.

I worry about my sisters, especially my youngest, and spend time distracting and entertaining them. When they get upset, I tell them to stop and offer an alternative activity that will cheer them up.

As I grow up, this doesn't change. In college, my finger is cut off in a sliding glass door accident, and before withdrawing from the semester for surgeries, I attend my psychology final exam. I complete it through throbbing pain with only one working hand. I get a 100 percent.

Later, when I get my heart broken, I immediately find a study abroad program to immerse myself in. I meet new best friends and see the world.

I don't know what to do with my life, so when I see an ad on the highway for a program that seems interesting, I set up an admissions interview by the following week.

My boss calls me into his office to say they have to reduce my salary by $10,000, and while I am already in overdraft, I quit my job that evening and start a business.

My son won't sleep and I am exhausted, but I spend the entire night researching the perfect school to enroll him in.

None of this is conscious to me—but when I look back, I can see the picture so clearly. In order to manage my own distress I lean into what is called eustress—positive, motivating stress that propels me forward.

People experience eustress when they feel confident about their ability to cope and solve problems. So, when I meet with couples in my office who continue to add more and more seemingly positive and productive things to their plate, I recognize it as a coping mechanism—"Something feels very, very wrong, so I am going to figure out how to make it feel right."

However, our eustress often encourages us to "Look over there . . . not here." When I read books or rearranged my room as a kid, I was able to cope with my dad and mom screaming at each other downstairs.

Many of us are stuck with an endless list of unsolvable, out-of-our-control problems—viruses, chronic illnesses, crime, financial crises, poor political leadership, lack of community connection, long hours at work, too much screen time, and civil unrest—so we pour extra stress into our cup by choice in order to have something to control.

Combine this with the fact that Western society has been telling people they can have it all for so long that we've all come to believe it. Books, social media, and podcasts encourage us to take on more and more. I open my Instagram feed and scroll through boss babes, Montessori moms, DIY dynamos, and financial freedom fighters. And as I watch their hyperbolic reels, I start to believe it—I can be all of those things too. Not only can I be . . . I *should* be.

Something strange has happened: the good type of stress—eustress—has somehow morphed into the bad kind of stress.

I understand what Ashley and Tyler are facing. As I would learn in later therapy sessions, they both had stressful childhoods and developed highly productive coping mechanisms. Their response to bad stress was to use good stress to get ahead—they played varsity sports, started clubs, and graduated at the tops of their classes. As they did this, they received messaging that it was good for them and encouragement to do more and shoot for the stars—even if getting to those stars meant racking up college debt that far exceeded the salary range of their chosen careers.

It makes sense that when they moved into their new home, it never felt like it measured up to the interior design work of Joanna Gaines. Meanwhile, blogs and Pinterest made it seem easy to replace their humble fiberglass tub with a vintage clawfoot bath. Even if it meant the associated expenses had to go on a credit card.

And I know Ashley isn't alone in the effort she has put into figuring out how to give her children the best education or taking care of an ailing parent. But she does this alongside everything else she does too. And it's just too much.

Moreover, Ashley and Tyler are feeling the pressure to do it all for their family, while also remaining relevant and social. They are waking up early on weekend mornings for their kids' sporting events and staying out late with friends in the evenings drinking too much wine.

Choosing to add stress and refusing to remove it is one of the biggest quagmires of our time. Our eyes are too big for our stomachs, but we try to eat it all anyway because we've convinced ourselves that having more will take away the tummy ache.

BRIDGING THE GAP BETWEEN FANTASY AND REALITY

By this time, Andrew and I have been married for a few years and we've taken on a lot. We have a dog, a child, a house, and a business. We try to maintain our hobbies, our health, and our friendships. But we also take on more. My husband joins a wedding band, and I decide to start sharing my relationship knowledge on Instagram. I sign up to volunteer with a mental health organization. I hire new employees for my practice.

Because we are living in my husband's hometown, there are endless opportunities for him to socialize with people he loves. Andrew is invited to join the local recreational softball team with all of his best friends from high school. We talk about it, and I encourage him to do it. "Are you sure?"

he asks. "I know you've been struggling and that you're tired at the end of the day."

I smile and nod. "I'm sure! It will be good for you!"

Twice a week, my husband comes home from work, gives me a kiss, throws on his softball gear, and runs out of the house while I seethe. I feel frustrated with myself for seething. *Why am I so upset?* I think. *This is who Andrew and I are! We are supportive of each other's hobbies.*

As time goes on, I start to create a story that his friends are at fault for his time away from the house. This narrative makes me less inclined to spend time with them, and when I do, I am less than enthusiastic.

I know that when you start blaming everyone else, it's a sign that it's time to take inventory on where you might be contributing to your own mess. Is it truly his friends who are the problem? Not really.

It's the gap—the distance between what we value, wish for, and believe in and what the reality of our lives can actually support. While in my heart of hearts I want to be the wife who supports her husband's recreational endeavors, I just can't be that person right now. It's painful to have to choose between your ideal and your reality, knowing that you might not be happy with either.

Like so many other Americans, bridging the gap between the type of spouse I want to be and the spouse I can actually be isn't the only gap I have to navigate. I am also trying to figure out the career-family gap. I have been led to believe that I can have it all. But recently I feel like that is a lie.

Every morning, I hug and kiss my baby goodbye and leave him in the arms of my mother or mother-in-law before rushing to my first appointment of the day.

When I attempt to bridge the gap between who I hope to be and who I am, I exhaust and demoralize myself. I take on more and more to hold up the bridge so that I don't have to admit any sort of defeat. But you can't escape reality—and the truth is that my bridge is falling down.

Tyler and Ashley's bridge is falling down too. Rather than removing the weight that was causing its collapse, they threw more money or time into solving the problem. They pay for food delivery since they don't have time to cook, hire outside help to take care of the kids in the evenings or over the weekends, and have someone clean the house.

What I was starting to notice, and what they would soon know to be true, is that so much of their life was about bridging the gap between fantasy and reality.

I believe my home should be perfect <u>AND</u> *we are a full-time working family that doesn't have the capacity to keep that up all the time.*

I believe our children should get all the love and care in the world <u>AND</u> *we have no energy for that.*

We love each other so much and want to be romantic toward each other <u>AND</u> *we leave absolutely no time to do it.*

I believe that to be a good daughter, I should be 100 percent involved in my mother's medical care <u>AND</u> *I am a full-time, working parent so I don't know how to fit it in.*

Ashley and Tyler bridged the gap by hemorrhaging money, outsourcing what really mattered to them, and drinking alcohol to avoid the lack of intimacy in their relationship. And to make ends meet, they worked more.

The hard part was helping Ashley and Tyler understand that their lives were stressful. That the stress was negatively impacting them and that things weren't going to get better until they stopped taking on so much. This was hard, because on paper, Tyler and Ashley had it good—"We are so lucky, though," they'd say. "We have so much."

And, of course, they do.

But they are miserable. We, as a society, are miserable.

These gaps are beautifully summed up by Beth Berry in her book *Motherwhelmed*, when she explores how frustrated we feel because of the gaps between our values, priorities, and desires and the reality of our resources and culture.[1]

Gaps like:

- I want to prioritize being with my children—it's most important to me—but my job penalizes me when I don't respond to my Slack messages immediately.

- I believe in a specific type of education for my children, but I don't have the money to pay for it and greater society judges me for wanting it.

- I believe in sustainable living, but between work, commuting, spending time with the people I love, and all my laundry, it's hard to be certain every purchase I make is sourced in the right way.

- I believe we should eat healthy, but the healthy food at the store is too expensive.

- I believe I should fight for social justice, but the administrative tasks of daily life leave me with no time to lean into what matters to me.

We feel these gaps and then observe other people supposedly filling them:

- The mom online who works the night shift but runs home during her breaks to rock her baby anyway.

- The parents who turned their entire home into Maria Montessori's dreamland, left their jobs, and now homeschool full-time.

- The friend who responds to all of their emails, WhatsApp messages, texts, Slacks, and direct messages, and still has time to work out, throw a party, and make dinner for their family.

- The successful career person who also advocates for everything they believe in. They speak out, go to conferences, attend the protests, and still seem to lean into their work, iron their clothing, and enjoy a vacation here and there.

It's not that gaps haven't existed before; it's that the gaps now are so visible because of marketing and technology and constant interconnectedness. We see our own gaps and then we see how other people bridge those gaps better than we do, thanks to the finely tuned algorithm. Before, people just had to accept their gaps and leave well enough alone.

With Ashley and Tyler, one of the first things we needed to uncover was the gap between what they had hoped would be their reality and what their reality actually was. I helped them start this conversation by journaling individually about the gaps they were feeling. I then moved them toward a conversation about how their need to bridge the gaps was impacting them.

"Being at the top of my career has always been incredibly important to me," Ashley shared. "But I also can't shake my desire to be more like my mom was. She was always there. She took us to all of our games, made us snacks in the afternoon, and read us books at night. I am constantly bridging the gap by either paying someone to do those things for our kids or by taking heat at work for limiting my hours there. It's exhausting, depressing, and creates so much guilt for me."

Ashley also shared her feelings of isolation—a belief that she is the only one who is failing *so miserably* at bridging all of the gaps in her life. She isn't alone. Behind the walls of the therapy room most people feel alone in what they deem to be their failings.

The reality is that I've never met anyone who is bridging these unrealistic gaps effectively.

And there is a plot twist: A lot of the gaps people perceive aren't the result of their own life philosophies. The gaps have been inherited subconsciously as people ingest messages from the people around them, capitalism, and media telling them what they should want and how they should look and live.

THE ILLNESS OF MORE, MORE, MORE

It is August 2013 and I am having a tough go of it. A crappy boyfriend, a crappy job, and crappy self-esteem have led me to the self-help section of Barnes & Noble. I'm looking at countless inspirational guides that promise to improve my life—most of which have some thread of "Do it all and don't be afraid." Or, as Tom and Donna from *Parks and Recreation* were saying at the time, "Treat yo' self."

I take it all in and decide, quite confidently, that I am going to have a year of yes, lean in, and treat myself. If an opportunity arises, I will take it! If there is a risk to be had, count me in!

And boy do I do it. I spend the next two months getting on dating websites, exercising, and starting a business. By October, I am proudly seeing clients who find me on a website I built from scratch in a Philadelphia Center City office, going on dates multiple days a week, and in the best shape of my life.

It is such a positive feedback loop that I continue to say yes, lean in, and take risks. My life is like an ever-expanding balloon. Every time I think that I can't possibly expand anymore, I make it work. I fit it all in.

I am glad I do. In fact, in the absence of any stress, I feel boredom. Learning a new skill, doing something even though it's hard, and exercising our bodies are all examples of good stress. With enough of it, I feel more social connection, focus, fun, curiosity, and motivation.

When Andrew and I get together, I maintain the same mindset. "We can make anything work as long as we roll up our sleeves and do it!" It's led us to our current predicament—too much work, too many obligations, and not enough time for each other.

We gain, gain, gain. But to what loss? More success at work resulted in less time with each other. A bigger house resulted in more yard work and less time to rest.

We make it all work, but over time, our eustress turns to distress, and it starts to wreak havoc on our health and family.

More, more, more is an illness. With more comes heightened arousal states. And as these get higher, what was once experienced as motivating and fun begins to be experienced as pressure. You'll become exhausted, burnt-out, overwhelmed, anxious, and even panicked. For every new thing you take on, you will need to find more ways to manage it. And more things to sacrifice so that you can.

WHEN IT'S NOT WORTH COMPROMISING WHAT MATTERS

I'm sitting on our IKEA couch hunched over my laptop as I search for affordable flights and hotels for a wedding we need to attend in just a few weeks. George's ex-nanny is getting married in Charleston, South Carolina, and she really wants us to come. She even asked George to be her ring bearer. As I look at one $800 flight after another, my heart begins to race. I've known for months that we can't afford to go, but I've lived in a delusion that I would figure it out. Since having a child, I've had to cut back on work. As a therapist, you only make money if you're seeing clients and so the reduction in clients has impacted our income. On top of that, I have just received a horrendous tax bill.

And, even if I could afford it, I would have to go alone with George. The wedding is on a Friday and Andrew has to work. Just the thought of getting on an airplane, going to a hotel, and celebrating a wedding solo with a toddler is causing me a great deal of anxiety.

As I Google flights, I work overtime, trying to figure out how to get there. *Maybe if I cut out the hotel cost and just go down Friday morning and come back Friday night we can afford it*, I think. Andrew sees the look on my face and interrupts my thought process. "Liz, you just have to tell her you can't go. We can't spend that money right now. You need to pay the tax bill."

"She will hate me," I respond.

"Let her," he says.

I cringe at his harsh response. I don't want her to hate me. I love her. I should have told her months ago that I couldn't go, and now this is all my fault. She is going to be angry. But Andrew is right. I don't want him to be, so I push back for a little while—I try to justify the expense and convince him we can do it.

"Liz, your family comes first. You come first. This is going to impact you and us negatively. Sometimes you have to disappoint people. You can't do it all."

I know he is right. If I go, it is going to burden the people I live with and cause unnecessary stress and conflict. I pick up the phone and get her voicemail. I leave an apologetic message letting her know I won't be able to come and that I am so sorry. I ask her to call me back when she's done with work. I tell her I want to celebrate in another way. She never calls me again.

She is mad, I am sure. I feel regret. And yet, I chose what was best for my family. I made a tough choice, but it was aligned with my most important value—peace and security with Andrew and George. Whenever I am working extra hard to justify something, I come back to what really matters and make the decision based on what is most important to me.

FINDING YOUR NORTH STAR

Sometimes, because of the forward momentum of life, we lose our North Star. We stop discussing where we are headed and start to feel lost. Tyler and Ashley had lost sight of their North Star. Every day they were making impulsive decisions driven by anxiety, fear, and comparison.

When Tyler comes to a session talking about a new property he is interested in buying, I have to stop him.

"Ashley, Tyler," I say in a very firm but friendly tone. "Where is this all headed?" They both search for answers, but "Umm . . . Uhhh . . ." is mostly what I hear.

"Each week, you come in with more and more added to your plate. Work, kids, hobbies, chores, people . . . there is always something being added. I want to pause and get clear on where you hope this is going to lead you in twenty years. What's the goal?"

"Early retirement," Tyler says. Ashley agrees.

"So why all the stuff?" I ask.

"It's going to help us be set up for success in the future."

"Not if it causes your divorce," I say with a smile.

They both laugh. I like working with them. It is easy to be honest and straightforward with Tyler and Ashley.

"Let's dig into what this is really all about. You both want to retire early, so you're doing all sorts of things—some of which are investments—but the other things are the tasks and expenses you have to take on to manage these investments."

I continue, "Why retire early—why is that important to you both?" It sounds like a commonsense question. Who doesn't want to retire early? I know I do. But I need to know which value it ties into for them.

"Well, I don't want to be working until I die," Tyler says.

Ashley shares, "I want to enjoy our grandkids. I want to be like my parents are to our kids."

"Can I share with you some inconsistencies I am seeing?" I ask. They nod.

I take a deep breath and run my fingers across the wood of my chair's armrest. I remind myself that they are the type of people I can be direct with.

"You don't want to work until you die, Tyler, but you're saving absolutely no money right now. You're totally in debt. You keep working more hours to cover it. Now you're making investments to cover other investments—a kind of 'rob Peter to pay Paul' scenario."

I look at Tyler with bated breath. No matter how long I do this, I still have an inner people pleaser and sometimes it can be hard to be direct. *Phew*, I think, *he's curious about what I'm saying but not mad.*

"Ashley, you really appreciate what your parents do for your kids, but you are still very hurt by what they didn't do for you. By being wrapped up in so much stress and activity every day, you're creating a scenario where you're not with your kids now so you can be with their kids later. It's continuing a pattern that you found painful."

Being the type A couple that they are, they thrive on feedback. "You're so right!" they both chime in. "How do we fix it?"

I help Ashley and Tyler look at the value behind their desire for early retirement. Tyler's dream to have fewer working years derives from his desire for a sense of freedom. Ashley's hope to have time for her grandkids is deeper than that. Her biggest dream is to live a lifestyle that allows her to have a sense of connection. Both of these goals can be worked toward now, not procrastinated on until later.

It's not only the privileged, like Ashley and Tyler, who lose their North Star under the constant need to do more and be more. There are couples across the United States who are putting Disney World trips on credit cards, planning over-the-top birthday parties, and buying their children brand-new Lululemon even though they can't afford it. They feel pressure to do these things because society makes them believe *everyone* is doing these things. And of course, each of us deserves pleasure, joy, and a little YOLO decision-making every now and then. But overall, we should be choosing where our energy and money go based on what actually matters to us, not what the world tells us matters to them.

We don't only do ourselves a favor when we get focused on what really matters, we do others a favor too by modeling a truth—we can't have and do it all, but our lives can still be good enough.

SESSION NOTES:

In this session, we explored the gaps between fantasy and reality, identified the "more, more, more" syndrome, and introduced the North Star. By combatting the "more, more, more" you will actually have *more* enjoyment in life and less self-created stress. By understanding your North Star, it will become easier to make decisions that are in alignment with where you want to go and what you actually want to have.

1. INTERVENTION: IDENTIFYING THE GAPS

What are the gaps between what you had hoped would be your reality and what your reality actually is? Write down those gaps and then explore how you try to bridge the gaps, even when it isn't good for you.

2. INTERVENTION: IDENTIFYING MORE, MORE, MORE

Where have you gotten caught up in "more"? Make a list of "more" you've taken on. Then, write out what you have had to sacrifice to make it work. For example, you might say you've signed up for another online course and in the exercise, you review the various costs associated with it. For example:

- Two hours of live class time a week, which means less time to just relax

- Five hundred dollars for the course, which means $500 less for the vacation you want to take with your partner next year, or $500 less of a cushion in your savings account

- Three hundred dollars for the materials, which means $300 less for the exercise classes you know make you feel better

- Two hours focusing on the material outside of class, which means two hours less to exercise and take care of the house

Perhaps you find this cost to be worth it, or perhaps you find that it doesn't align with what really matters to you in the big picture.

3. INTERVENTION: THE NORTH STAR

Talk to your partner about what matters most to both of you in life. An easy way to think about this is to ask the question, "At the end of life, where will we want to be? Who do we want to be? And what do we hope we've done?"

Your North Star is often motivated by your values. For example, if you value family, you should be utilizing the North Star of family in decision-making by asking yourself, *Is the decision I am making here aligning with my goal of being a family person?*

CHAPTER 6

Lean into the Good Enough Life

I wake up on March 21, 2020, at 6:00 am to get my family ready for the day—making breakfast, packing lunches, getting myself dressed, and checking early morning emails—followed by rushing my son to school and hopping on an hour-long train ride to the city for work.

This morning is like many others before it. Stressful, messy, rushed, and overwhelming. The afternoons that follow are heavy on me too. Being a CEO in the workplace and a CEO at home mean I am a master delegator, rememberer, task undertaker, and boo-boo kisser.

Many days I wonder how much longer I can take it. Things have started to improve. Andrew and I have gotten so much better at self-soothing and delegating the mental load. We are more mindful of what we take on. And yet, I still feel angry that regardless of how much we have tried to redistribute stress in our lives, it still seems to fall on me. I am trying so hard to be a perfect mother that I overextend myself. My husband works from 9:00 am to 6:00 pm, but because I want to pick up my son from school, I squish my work between the hours of 9:00 am and 2:00 pm.

But the afternoon of March 21 is different. Halfway through the day, my phone starts lighting up. The world is closing. Initially, for two weeks. Then, two more weeks. Then, two years.

On this day, my relationship with work and life in general starts to face a reckoning. And so does my husband's.

WHEN THE HUSTLER CAN'T HUSTLE

"Go, go, go" is the message we get from society. You've got one life to live and you need to live it. Don't stop. Do more. Climb the ladder, get the fit body, travel the world. Keep the house together. Learn more.

And if you've got a quiet moment? Well, you better find something to do with it. Go through the cabinets and get rid of old spices. Empty the dishwasher. Watch a webinar. Don't spend a moment without being productive.

We live in a constant state of survival mode. It's as if we are run by a motor that thinks, *I can't stop! If I do, something very bad will happen!* And yet we really don't ask ourselves what that bad thing is.

Living in this stressed state becomes addictive. It becomes the only way we know how to be.

And when we can't be in that state, it can feel at the very least disconcerting and at the worst panic inducing.

When the pandemic shut down my life, I no longer had to run to George's school and then the train and then the office. I couldn't take George to the library or swimming classes. I wasn't able to go to Home Depot to start a home renovation project. The gym was closed.

My life of go, go, go suddenly turned into a life that was slow, slow, slow.

At first, I didn't know what to do with that. I found new ways to be busy. I scheduled more clients than I usually would, I found some seed packets in a drawer and started a garden in the backyard, I cleared out our living room and made it look like George's Montessori school.

I fought the slow.

So did most everyone else. TikTok became a representation of the frantic need to fill the space with something—it seemed like everyone was either dancing or baking.

As a therapist, I was witnessing this not only in myself, but in my clients. After a few weeks, I had to check in with what was going on. Of course our reaction made so much sense—our stress response to the worldwide threat of the pandemic was kicked into gear, but there was nowhere to run, no one to fight. We used our activation to do other things.

I knew, though, that the act of doing provided a false sense of security, and it wasn't sustainable for the health of my clients (or myself). In order to effectively move out of the stress cycle, we needed to allow ourselves to move into a space of restoration.

If people don't allow themselves to recover, they become burnt-out, physically and mentally ill, and their relationships suffer. We just aren't meant to live in our stress.

Restoration means slowing down, being quiet, and reconnecting with our values. It means allowing things to be good enough. I realized, though, that I had no idea how to do that. No matter how much I preached it to my clients, struggled to do it myself. The time of forced solitude during the start of the pandemic allowed me to come face to face with this and to begin to explore what it would mean to let things be good enough.

Client Profile

Bria (32/F) is recently single and living alone in her Philadelphia apartment. She originally came to therapy to discuss a breakup and an anxiety disorder, and is currently in maintenance therapy after working with me for about a year.

It's a few weeks into the pandemic, and I am having a therapy session with a long-term client. Bria, a young woman with a zest for life, had been meeting with me for over a year. Initially, she came in to navigate a breakup and some anxiety, but now she comes infrequently for check-ins. Usually, Bria and I would meet in my office. She'd bound into the room after a brief jog from her apartment and immediately jump into sharing with me the tales of her life. Today, though, we are meeting through a screen.

Before this week, I didn't even have a "home office." It should have been easy enough in our four-bedroom home to turn one of the rooms into an office, but both my sister and cousin have been displaced by the pandemic and are living in the extra rooms.

I spend time moving the bed in our bedroom against the wall so that the view from the camera will show a blank wall behind me. I take a kitchen chair and place it in front of the dresser. I open my laptop and am testing the video quality when I notice the room is far too dark. I look like . . . a hostage. With only two minutes until the start of the session, I scramble to open the blinds and get some more light into the room. Finally, I sit down and click "start" on our session.

"Hi, Bria! It's so good to see you! How are you doing?"

Bria, who is sitting on her bed with a pile of pillows behind her, is looking at me with sad eyes. "Oh no," I say. "I can see something has happened. Bria, what's going on?"

Tears are starting to stream down her face as she mutters, "I have cancer. Stage 4."

I'm shocked. I know everything about Bria and not once have we discussed any worries about her health. My heart is beating and I want to cry. My mind is racing to my sister-in-law, Sam, who is in the midst of her own cancer treatment. I swallow and inhale to keep the tears back behind my eyes where they belong.

"When did you find out?"

"This morning . . . and my own mother wasn't even allowed to come into the room with me. I had to do it alone." Then, in a very recognizable use of coping mechanisms, she waves her hands in front of her face "brushing away" her tears, smiles, laughs, and says, "At least my mask was there to hug my face!"

I smile back because I recognize that she needs some brevity and that sitting in the pain really is just too much right now. I am starting to feel angry—angry for Bria, that her mom wasn't able to be in the appointment with her, and angry that I can't be in an in-person session with Bria right now. I can't do much through a screen, but if we were meeting in person, I could hand her a tissue or even give her a hug.

Since I can tell Bria would rather us speak "intellectually" about the subject, I ask her for details. "What did they say?" Bria starts telling me what the doctor shared and the course of treatment. As she does, I can't ignore the parallel in my own life. My sister-in-law, Sam, is also facing cancer treatments. Pre-pandemic, she had friends and family by her side at every appointment and now she sits alone in cold rooms being hugged by only a mask, too.

Liz, Bria . . . Bria is the focus here. Go back to her, I remind myself when I notice that I am getting distracted by my own thoughts. Just as I return to being fully present with Bria, I hear a noise from downstairs.

Not just a noise . . . but wailing.

It's George. "Mommy! Mommy! Why are you working? Please come down! MOMMY." It isn't a demand; it's a plea. He sounds desperate for me to come downstairs and be with him. His voice is cracking and he's having a difficult time breathing through his tears.

George has been struggling deeply with the major adjustments to our life due to the lockdown. He misses his Montessori school, he feels afraid of the "ow-side" ("Mommy, people awen't suspost go out thewe anymowe," he says, without his *r's*), and he needs a lot of soothing. Bria needed her mom to hug her during her moment of pain . . . but where is George's mom when he needs the same thing?

My chest is getting tight and heavy, my breathing shallow, and I feel frozen. *How can I be here for all of these people right now? What the hell am I supposed to do for Sam? How can I hold space for Bria? What can I do to let George know I am here for him?*

I want to cry—for Bria and her fear, for George and his confusion, for Sam and her loneliness, and for me and my overwhelm.

I also want to scream. *Why isn't Andrew doing anything!* I start to rage in my mind.

I let Bria know that I need to take a moment. She looks at me, taken aback. I can tell she is annoyed and now I feel even worse. *I'm a terrible therapist*, I think.

I mute the mic and turn off the video on my laptop and quickly type (bang) out a message to Andrew:

"What the hell is happening! I am working! Why aren't you dealing with George? What is wrong with you?"

I delete it. *Deep breaths, Liz. Deep breaths. Remember, when you get anxious, you start to get critical. You're anxious right now. Write it a different way.* I am using a technique that I teach my therapy clients to stop the spiral. The technique, which is called *name it to tame it*, is proven to help people soothe difficult emotions that might lead them into undesirable behavioral patterns.

After I take my deep breaths, I type out another message using non-violent communication—another skill I teach couples. I am trying to walk the talk even though it's hard.

"Babe, I hear George downstairs. I am really overwhelmed. I need help. Can you soothe him?"

Andrew, though, is in just as much of a pickle as I am. His boss, Ian, just sent him a Slack message demanding that he hop on a call, pronto.

Having watched half of his colleagues get laid off since lockdown measures were taken, I know Andrew doesn't feel safe enough to let his boss know that he won't be free until I am finished with my session. My phone lights up with a message from him:

"I am doing my best. I don't know what to do. Ian made me get on a call. George is so upset and screaming in the background. Literally don't know what to do."

I don't know what to do either. I have a responsibility to Bria professionally, but she is also personally important to me. I care about her deeply. I've known her for years. I see her more often than I see some of my friends. I need to be here for her.

But, I also have a responsibility to George. He is struggling. He needs his mommy and daddy. He is dealing with big and messy feelings during a big and messy time. He is little, and so confused.

When I am stressed, I tend to lend myself to blame. I want to blame Andrew so badly. But how can I? These stressors have absolutely nothing to do with the issues that we have faced in the past. Andrew and I are both doing our best, but our best isn't enough.

I take another deep breath . . . *in through my nose and out through my mouth*. I turn the session with Bria back on and we continue our work together. George continues to cry and I do my best.

The session ends and I walk downstairs. The blinds are all closed and the room smells thick from the number of people packed into the house working and stressing all day.

Andrew is hunched over at the kitchen table. He has a look of stress and defeat—shoulders slumped, head in his hands—as he continues to talk to Ian about major losses in revenue since the lockdown. I give him a sympathetic smile and turn to look toward George.

George is sitting near Andrew, wet-faced and exhausted. "Mommy, why didn't you come? Why are you and Daddy always working? Why am I not at my schoooooool."

The last word is drawn out beneath tears and sniffles. He is so sad, so disappointed, and so hurt. I have to cancel the day; that's all there is to it.

I email my clients to let them know I need to reschedule their appointments. I sit with George on the couch, cuddling and rocking him until he falls asleep. I am thinking about all of the ways in which I am failing my family and my clients. I notice that I feel afraid for the future. *What if Andrew loses his job? What if I can't see the number of clients I need to make ends meet?*

I give George a kiss on the top of his head, brush his hair back with my fingers, and walk him up the stairs to this room. I snuggle him in a blanket on the chair and dim the lights. Then, I pick up my phone.

There's an email notification from Bria:

> Hi Liz,
>
> I wanted to write to let you know I was very disappointed in our session today. I was sharing something important with you and you did not seem like yourself. You seemed distracted the entire time. I couldn't tell if you were truly listening. I know this isn't the norm, so I wanted to let you know I felt hurt.
>
> Bria

I put my phone down and take another deep breath. I give George another kiss and stand up, swaying with him around the room. I'm crying quietly as I look at him. His little eyes are closed so gently, his wet eyelashes showing evidence of his tears.

I put him down in his bed and wander to my room/office. I lie down on the recently rearranged bed and close my eyes. I'm still crying, but now it's more audible. My family and the clients I work with are among the most important people in my life. I care deeply for them. I'm devastated to hear about what is happening to Bria. Because of my stress, I wasn't able to be present for her the way she needed. No matter how hard I had tried to be centered and calm, I just wasn't.

I wrote her back:

> Dear Bria,
>
> I am so sorry. You are right. I was distracted and not there for you in the right way. I won't charge you for today and let's reschedule as soon as possible so I can

give you the time, space, and support you absolutely deserve. I hope you'll give me an opportunity to make this right.

I am here for you,

Liz

I turn on the TV to images of helicopters flying over Philadelphia, people being pulled out of cars, and buildings on fire. I can't take it, so I turn off the TV. I open Instagram and check my direct messages.

"Did you know you have a typo in one of your posts?"

"You wrote something that I don't agree with. Do you even do your research?"

"How could you post something like that when a pandemic is going on? Why haven't you been posting about getting people to stay indoors? You're so irresponsible with your platform!!"

"LOL. YOU WRITE THE DUMBEST SHIT."

"Why haven't you posted about the protests in Philly yet and what you believe?! You're complicit in harm!"

Just kill me, I think, *I can't do anything right.*
Here are the gaps again. I have been passionate about social justice for my entire life. In my teens and twenties I was outspoken. I took on volunteer roles, I protested, I wrote Facebook posts that shared exactly what I thought, I donated money, and I pushed myself to learn more and be better.

Social justice is something that matters to me. And the gap between what I want to do and what I am able to do seems to be growing more and more every day.

If I was talking to a client, I would tell them to have compassion for themselves. Running a business and making sure my employees don't get laid off, homeschooling my son, and supporting my clients in the therapy room doesn't leave a lot of space for all of the other things that could be said or done. I am doing enough.

But today, I hate myself for it. My nervous system is dysregulated and I don't know how to calm it down.

Eventually, Andrew gets into bed next to me. "I found out that Ian let my brother go today. And in the morning, I have to tell Jeff he is being let go too. I feel like I am failing everyone."

I take a moment to talk to Ian in my head, *Who the fuck lets the guy whose wife has cancer go? And during a pandemic? Fuck you.*

"Me too," I say.

"Something needs to change with our jobs."

"I agree. This isn't going to work."

I say this in unison with millions of other moms across the globe. Two million of whom I would later find out left the workplace completely during that time.

Little did I know that this was the start of a journey that would change the way we allowed stress to infiltrate our family. Things were going to change in both big and small ways. We cuddle in bed until we both fall asleep, exhausted from the stress hormones pumping through our bodies day after day.

KEEPING UP WITH @THEJONESES

In the early 1900s, Arthur Mormand created a comic strip called *Keeping Up with the Joneses*. The comic focused on a family that was driven to obsessively consume more in order to keep up with a named, but never seen, neighbor: the Joneses. In today's world, we'd know them as @thejoneses.

The creator of the comic admitted that his life was the source material—he and his wife spent a great deal of money and energy trying to keep up with the wealth they saw around them.

While the Mormands were struggling to wear wonderful clothes and get something out of life like the mysteriously wealthy Jones family, so are we today.

We want so much, so we work so much. And then we don't have the time or energy for what we really want deep down inside—relationships.

For my husband and I, the pandemic was our come-to-Jesus moment—helping us to see all the ways in which we were trying to keep up with who knows who. Our career aspirations, the way in which we used our time, gave our energy, and spent our money wasn't really aligned with our North Star. All of these things took us far away from each other, making it harder to deal with the stressors we couldn't control—a pandemic, cancer in the family, and other daily frustrations. We were at each other's throat, but it didn't need to be this way.

We started to check in with ourselves—did we really need any of this? Did we really want to do any of this?

We didn't need to keep up with the Joneses. We needed to close our laptops, turn off our phones, and keep up with the little boy who was struggling so deeply.

DITCHING HUSTLE CULTURE

The pandemic was the kick in the rear I needed to start living a good enough life. A good enough life is, simply put, good enough. For so long, I was trying to be excellent. "You only live once! Live big!" But what I've come to find, alongside my husband, is that you only live once so you should live well.

In 1953, Donald Winnicott, a pediatrician and psychoanalyst, coined the phrase, the good enough mother. The good enough mother is exactly what it sounds like—a mother who is good enough. She doesn't need to be perfect because her children are imperfect themselves. A good enough mother tries her best—she is loving and responsive most of the time, but sometimes she slacks. Sometimes she misses the mark.

Decades later, we still struggle to remind mothers that they need to lean into being good enough, not perfect. Beyond mothering, though, good enough is enough in every area of life.

Learning to be good enough at our jobs, our friendships, and our partnerships should be the ideal. And yet, it isn't. We pore over parenting books, we lean into hustle culture, we over-analyze the right way to be a friend or a partner. We spend time, energy, and money on perfect bodies, houses, and experiences for our children.

Learning to be good enough isn't easy. We are constantly inundated with outside messages asking us to be *more*. Because of this, you have to make a conscious and disciplined decision to let *enough be enough*. This small shift in my own thinking has made a tremendous difference in my life. I am not always striving, but we, as a family, are still thriving.

Being good enough means allowing your stress cycle to resolve and to recognize your constant movement is about being stressed and to instead choose rest. Choosing rest means taking a breath, being mindful of the world around you, and connecting with the people you love.

Perhaps my husband and I wouldn't climb to the top of the career ladder, but we would have more time at home with each other. Perhaps we couldn't go on a million vacations a year, but we'd have financial security. Maybe we'd have to step back from some hobbies for a little while, but we'd both have enough time to dedicate to keeping our home a peaceful place. First, we would need to understand which parts of the horrible stress we could control and what to do when we couldn't control it at all.

NAVIGATING WHAT YOU CAN'T CONTROL

It's warm outside and my husband and I are rushing down the street to meet a large group of friends to celebrate Sam and Dan. Dan is my brother-in-law—my husband's twin to be exact—and Sam is my soon-to-be sister-in-law. She is tiny in every way and has long, beautiful blonde hair. To make up for her short stature, she wears the highest of high heels everywhere she goes in rain, wind, or snow. They are having a destination wedding in just a few weeks, and tonight we are celebrating the fact that they got their marriage license in the courthouse that afternoon.

As we walk into the bar, we give our friends a hug and I look around to find Sam. I see her standing next to Danielle, whispering about something. I walk over and give an apprehensive look—I don't want to interrupt a private conversation, but they invite me in.

"Liz, come here . . ." Sam says. "I don't want you to say anything to anyone, no need for people to be upset, but can you feel this lump for me? Right here . . . does it feel weird to you?" She lifts her arm and points to a spot between her breast and her armpit. I pull down her white dress a bit to feel it.

My stomach drops. I don't know what breast cancer feels like, but if I did, I would imagine it feels like this. It doesn't feel like a mass of tissue; it feels like a pebble. A rock.

I look at Danielle. "You should feel it," I say. As Danielle touches the lump, I can tell from her face that she is worried too. We lift Sam's dress back up, zip it, and put her hair back into place. "Do you have an appointment to get it looked at?" I ask. "I do, but after the wedding," she says. "The doctor doesn't want to ruin our big day for no reason."

I know at that moment that Sam has cancer. "You're going to be okay," I say. We spent the rest of the night drinking with our friends and celebrating their commitment to each other.

Sam and Dan have their big day. We celebrate them at a beach resort in Mexico, working hard to relegate our worries about the lump to the back of our minds as we go through the motions of a wedding.

A few days after we get home, Sam asks Andrew and I to come over. "The doctor is calling me soon and I don't want us to be alone."

We head over to Sam's house to be with her while she waits for the phone call. She gets it and it's confirmed—cancer.

On the way home, Andrew and I sit quietly. We walk into our messy house, pick up our son from the sitter's arms, and have her go home for the evening. The fridge is essentially empty. Sheets aren't on the bed. We are winging it every day.

As we stand in the kitchen trying to figure out what to make ourselves for dinner, I look at him and say, "I really hope they are taking this seriously." My tone is abrasive and accusatory . . . toward whom I am not sure.

Stop talking, I think, *What you're saying serves no one right now. Be gentle.* I keep my grouchy face on anyway.

Clearly, the stress from hearing the news and walking into a disorganized home is flooding my body.

My husband responds, "What's your problem? I'm not going to sit here and listen to you be like this," he says as he walks away. He is also flooded with stress hormones. Neither of us know how to respond to this, so we bicker on and off the rest of the night.

Stress doesn't only come from the choices we make—taking on more hours at work, spending too much money on unnecessary things, or signing up for every possible obligation. It also comes from many, many things in which we were never granted any choice at all; the only option we have is to learn how to cope without turning on each other.

> ### Couple Profile
>
> Harvey (36/M) and Lisa (38/F) have tried to have a child for the last three years. They've experienced three pregnancy losses, including one at six months. Harvey owns a realty firm and Lisa is in pharmaceutical sales. They come to therapy to "fix their grief."

I'm crying in a therapy session and I am having a hard time stopping. But it's not my therapy session; it's Harvey and Lisa's. Harvey and Lisa are clients of mine, and today they are sharing with me that they've lost their pregnancy . . . again. In the year that I've seen them, they've experienced three losses, the first at six weeks, the second at six months, and this loss at three months.

Harvey, a gentle and soft-spoken man, wraps his arm around Lisa. She's crying too. The office is inappropriately cheery and bright as the afternoon sun pierces through the window. We are all silent. The past year has been traumatic for the couple, and today feels hopeless.

I feel embarrassed that I'm crying. As a therapist, I hear a lot of sad stories and I'm trained to handle it. But something about Harvey and Lisa's pain is impacting me deeply.

I want to apologize for crying during their therapy session, but instead, I let them know how their story is making me feel. I know they have felt isolated from others and at times don't think their friends and family really understand the level of distress the pregnancy losses have caused. "To them," Lisa had shared in a previous session, "it's just a blip. A pregnancy, not a baby."

I look at them and instead of apologizing, I say, "We are all crying here. This is an incredibly painful experience the two of you are having, and I can see that and feel it as your witness."

"Something about seeing you cry, Liz, helps me to know that I am not crazy," Lisa says, as she grabs another tissue from the table across from her and dabs her face. "I've felt so alone. Like I am going through the worst time in my life and no one cares. No one except for Harvey . . . and you."

After providing thousands of hours of therapy I have learned that sometimes it can have a profound effect on how lonely someone feels just to know that at least one other person has been moved by their story.

"I'm at a loss," Lisa says. "I just don't even know how to get through this."

Harvey looks at me. "Just tell me how to make it better for her please. Just anything. I'll do anything."

He takes his hand and firmly presses her shoulder, a loving and protective gesture. His brows are furrowed, his eyes are glassy, and tears are running down his cheeks.

Harvey is devastated about the impact this is having on Lisa.

As I look at him, I wish I had an answer. There isn't an easy one. This event is so totally out of their control, and it is normal for both Lisa and Harvey to be in distress. I know he isn't going to be able to take away her grief.

"There is nothing we can do, Harvey. Nothing," Lisa says. "This just keeps happening to us! Stop asking what you can do. I give up. You should too." Lisa's shoulders slump as she picks at her cuticles. She is looking to me to validate her in her hopelessness.

Beside her, though, her partner sits straight and tall. He wants to help her and believes there must be a way. He is looking to me to give him the key to resolving her distress.

When experiencing pain, we often come face-to-face with our own beliefs about control. We either believe we can do something to change the stress—known in psychology as an internal locus of control—or we believe we can't do anything and that the outside world will make our choices for us—this is called an external locus of control.

Right now, Harvey believes that there has to be something he can do to make this situation feel better and to protect Lisa. If he just works hard enough, he will say the right words, take her to the right doctor, and find the path forward.

Lisa, on the other hand, feels completely defeated. This is just something that happens to them, she thinks, there is nothing they can do. She believes that there are no words to say, no actions to take, and no path forward.

Both have a very different idea about control. In my work with couples, I often have to help them reality check what they do and don't have control over and help them accept that.

"Harvey," I say gently. "I know you want to help Lisa. I know that all these questions and information seeking are ways for you to gain some sense of control. I want to help you have that sense of control in your life with Lisa. Lisa, I also want you to feel some control too."

I can't help but relate to Harvey. It's hard for me not to have the answers to suffering too. My husband and I are arguing a lot at home because I keep giving too many suggestions for dealing with my sister-in-law's cancer diagnosis. If I can get my husband to solve the issues Sam and Dan are facing, then everything will be okay.

I look over at Lisa. Her arms are crossed over her stomach and her shoulders are slouched. Her beautiful brown hair is matted on her wet cheeks. I take a sip of water and continue.

"You have to find control where it realistically exists and you have to be willing to find some acceptance where it doesn't exist. Harvey, you can't control how Lisa feels right now. Nothing you say or do is going to make it better. And I am sure it's frustrating that the doctors can't tell you what to do either. I think if you could accept that and listen to Lisa's grief around that reality, things would be better for her and for you."

A lot of my work is helping people who have a strong internal locus of control understand that while they might be very good at solving most problems, some just can't be solved. Not everything is figure-out-able. At this moment, I know that Lisa would feel comforted if Harvey could just admit that.

I pause for a moment and let Harvey take in what I've said. I take a sip of water and then turn my body toward Lisa.

"Lisa, you're right. There is nothing that can be done about the pregnancy loss. That is why it's so painful. Right now, you just want Harvey to accept that."

Lisa looks up at me and nods her head. "That's all I want," she says as she starts to cry more. "I just want him to understand that nothing can be done. I am just sad. Can't he just be sad too?"

She looks at him as she says this and he scoots closer to her and gives her a big hug. Lisa falls into his arms, allowing all of her muscles to go limp as she continues to cry. It's clear he's taken in what I've said as he quietly holds her. Maybe I need to take my own advice too, and just allow my husband to feel every now and then. No solutions necessary.

I allow them to be this way together for a few minutes. After Lisa has reached a catharsis, she sits up, crosses her legs, and grabs a tissue. She starts dabbing her face as Harvey continues to hold her hand. I inhale and continue.

"Harvey, there are a lot of things you can't do in this situation. But there are also some things you can do. Let's start to focus on what you can control."

I go on to explain to Harvey that right now he could empower himself by learning how to be a supportive listener by not rushing to solutions. Instead, he can show Lisa he understands the reality of the situation by offering validation, support, and affection, and by asking good questions.

"It seems like you're doing a pretty good job of that right now," I say to him. "What do you think, Lisa?"

"I agree. This is really all I need from you. Just hugs and support and not trying to fix it all."

Harvey squeezes her hand and responds, "You're right. There is nothing I can do. I'm sorry I keep pushing."

In that moment, Lisa exhales a lot of the stress she's been carrying all this time.

CONTROL

There is both an internal and external locus of control. An internal locus of control is when we believe that we can take steps to change our circumstances. An external locus of control is when we believe everything is left to the wind—and it's not in our control where the wind blows.

When we have things in our lives that cannot, at their core, be changed, we have to be able to hold both an internal and external locus of control. The external locus of control is giving ourselves permission to accept that there is nothing we can do to change the scenario and nothing we did to cause it. It might sound like:

- Our house burnt down and there was nothing I could have done to prevent it and nothing I can do to get it back. This was caused by something outside of me.

- Our child is sick and there was nothing I could have done to prevent it. This was caused by a genetic condition.

- My partner is experiencing postpartum depression. There is nothing they did to cause this. It is caused by hormonal shifts.

We have to hold these thoughts alongside the thoughts that come with a strong internal locus of control. We have to remember where our power is within the situations we cannot change. This might sound like:

- Yes, our house burnt down and there is nothing I can do to change that. And, I can start to call our insurance company to find out next steps.

- Yes, my child is sick and I could not have prevented it. And, I do have the power to increase their comfort by feeding them well, helping them to rest, and giving them a lot of love.

- Yes, my partner is depressed and much of it is in response to hormonal shifts. And, I can absolutely support them by making it easier for them to attend therapy appointments, taking stress off their plate, and being connected to them as much as possible.

When people are forced to adapt to unfair life scenarios, the ability to combine the internal and external locus of control improves your compassion for yourself and others and increases the likelihood of problem-solving. This means you are better able to see the reality of suffering and still feel moved to improve it from a place of empowerment rather than being stuck in a place of bitterness.

COPING STRATEGIES

The word *cope* comes from the Old French word *couper*, which means to come to blows with. Synonyms of cope are contend, deal, get by, grapple, make do, and manage.[1] Sometimes, the best we can do is cope with the cards we've been dealt—whether it be a temporary or long-term hand. Coping usually isn't pretty. Coping helps us get through to the other side. When done well, it also helps us make room for peace, joy, and fulfillment in an otherwise overwhelming life.

Sometimes, we cope by using unhealthy coping strategies like distancing ourselves from loved ones, picking fights, or partaking in activities that make us sick (socially, emotionally, or physically). However, we can all learn to adapt in ways that lift us up rather than tear us down.

Mindful coping requires us to focus on routines, rituals, and practices that help create safety, predictability, and restoration within our life. As Esther Perel says, "Routines get us through the day. Rituals guide us through life."[2] Practices help us do both.

A coping practice is something we do to help ourselves feel more grounded and in less pain. These practices include deep breathing, progressive muscle relaxation, journaling, mindfulness, exercise, and social touch. Social touch is when we reach for connection and receive connection back. We can experience this through something brief, like a check-in text, or something longer, like a coffee date with a reliable friend.

When we have the ability to tap into something like deep breathing or exercise to help our bodies feel less emotional or physical pain, even if temporarily, we can begin to commit to routines and rituals that will get us through life in a way that supports healing and regulation.

Routines are the tasks we complete each day. For the sake of this book, they are tasks that improve our well-being. Brushing our teeth when we wake up, taking out the trash before we leave the house, and making sure we eat something before we get started on our day are all examples of routines. They tend to be boring, but are important when it comes to taking care of ourselves and creating a cadence to daily life. They also provide us with a sense of control, which can be important when navigating out-of-control experiences.

Rituals are like routines except they carry meaning. For example, it might be routine to pack your lunch each morning but could become a ritual to do the task with a special brew of coffee. It may be routine to wash your face before bed, but a ritual if afterward, you and your partner always snuggle up and kiss each other's fresh-cleaned skin.

Some rituals happen frequently; for example, my husband and I drink coffee together almost every morning. Others happen with less frequency—like celebrating special holidays and birthdays—and some with even less frequency—like how we celebrate a marriage, graduation, or the birth of a baby, or memorialize someone at a funeral.

Individuals can combat their stress by honoring both routine and rituals, even when it's hard (remember, it's okay to do them imperfectly). Partnerships become stronger through routine and ritual. Doing both requires intentionality and mindfulness. When families, whether they are comprised of two or twenty people, have rituals and routines, they can stay at the helm of their own ship.

As William Doherty, the author of *The Intentional Family*, shares, "an Intentional Family is one whose members create a working plan for maintaining and building family ties and then implement the plan as best they can. An Intentional Family rows and steers its boat rather than being moved only by the winds and the current." In his book, he also discusses how families who have rituals and routines are less likely to lean into unhealthy coping mechanisms during hard times. In my office, the couples who have routines and rituals are less likely to slide into overspending, overdrinking, or too much screen time.[3]

After Lisa and Harvey spent some time with their initial grief, they knew they needed to add more structure to their lives. "I can't just keep laying on the couch feeling sorry for myself," Lisa shares. "I just end up hurting myself more by looking up research papers that tell me all of the things I don't want to hear. I need something to look forward to."

Harvey takes her hand and says, "How about that vacation we've been planning, Lis?" I smile at Harvey. A vacation does sound nice. It might be part of what Lisa needs. But I stop them.

"Harvey, Lisa, before planning the vacation, let's talk about day-to-day life. Often, people go on vacations to feel better about a life they want to run from. There is nothing wrong with that type of relief, but I also don't want you to return from the vacation to a daily life that still feels . . . awful."

"It's true. I feel like anytime we go on a vacation after something bad happens, everything is all good while we are away, but when we come back, it's just the same—or even worse—then how we left it," Lisa says. Harvey nods his head.

I talk to them about the importance of building practices into their daily life that can give them the power to combat stress. We explore what feels helpful to them both—for Lisa, exercise is always a regulating force, while Harvey absolutely hates it. He prefers to spend time in quiet, thinking and breathing. I ask them to commit to focusing on just one practice that helps them, and they agree that over the week they'll make it a point to exercise and take time for quiet reflection. From there, I move on. "Share with me your daily routines . . . what are the things you do each day without missing a beat?"

Harvey and Lisa share that they think they've let a lot of their routines slip. They used to pack their lunches, but now they've been ordering out. Lisa used to get up, shower, and follow a hair routine, but recently, she's just been throwing it in a ponytail and using a lot of dry shampoo. "My type of girl." I smile. "I have never been the type of person to get up and give myself a blowout, but it sounds like that routine was, at one time, important to you. Would you like to get back to it?"

Lisa nods her head. She sighs and shares that getting ready for the day helps her to feel empowered, as if she can take on anything.

I don't want them to become overwhelmed, so I ask them to focus on reintegrating just a few very easy, very boring routines back into their daily life. They agree to start packing lunches again and to wake up a bit earlier so they can get a little more dressed up for work. *That's my personal hell*, I think, *but to each their own.*

I continue to rituals. "What about connection—what do you do to connect with each other?"

"Sometimes we watch TV," Harvey chimes in.

"I would hardly call that connecting," Lisa responds.

"Why not?" I ask her.

She goes on to tell me that when they watch TV, at least one of them is on their phone and likely the other is on a laptop responding to emails. They are beside each other, but not connecting.

"Rituals of connection can be really simple, you know. I don't want you to overwhelm yourselves. What if you started packing lunch together in the morning? You could make your routine become a special time where you talk and are present with each other."

Harvey and Lisa leave their session with a plan. It hasn't changed their painful experience, but it has created structure and predictability and has given them a bit of control in an out-of-their-control situation.

SESSION NOTES:

In the previous session, we focused on the North Star and making decisions that are in alignment with it. In this session, we focused on the idea of control. Some stress is within our control to change, while other stress is out of our control. Life is messy and sometimes things happen that we can't change or prepare ourselves for. We learned about locus of control, the importance of accepting when you can't solve a problem and leading with empathy, and how to build coping skills. The following interventions will help you navigate life when the water gets rough.

1. INTERVENTION: MERGING THE INTERNAL AND EXTERNAL LOCUS OF CONTROL

When you face a difficult situation, challenge yourself to use the word *and* to combine both internal and external locus of control thoughts. The external locus of control involves giving ourselves permission to accept that there is nothing we can do to change the scenario and nothing we did to cause it. The internal locus of control is remembering where our power is within a situation we cannot change. For example, "My credit card payment is late and the company keeps calling me. I know I have a responsibility and the ability to figure out the solution to paying it (internal locus of control), AND I also understand that the tree falling on our house and causing the major roof expense was outside of my control (external locus of control)."

2. INTERVENTION: ACCEPT THAT YOU CAN'T SOLVE THE PROBLEM

Learning to accept that there are some problems you can't solve (at least not right now) will make you a better, more empathetic, and more present partner. Sometimes, the lemons are so rotten that no matter how hard you try, you cannot make lemonade.

3. INTERVENTION: LISTEN WITH EMPATHY WHEN THINGS AREN'T SOLVABLE

Listening with empathy requires:

- Letting go of your obligation to fix the issue

- Recognizing that your presence is not only enough, but all that can be given in the moment

- Avoiding platitudes and silver linings

- Looking for the feelings instead of the solutions (for example, saying "I can see you're so hurt," instead of, "How can I fix that for you?")

- Providing a space for your partner to express themselves

4. INTERVENTION: MINDFUL COPING

Circle two of the coping practices below that you can focus on over the next few weeks. Then, come up with two routines (daily practices for self-care) and two rituals (meaningful, repetitive practices for self-relational fulfillment) that you can begin to utilize to bring a sense of safety and groundedness into an otherwise overwhelming life.

Practices

- Journaling

- Exercise

- Breathing

- Reflection

- Mindfulness

- Social touch

Routines

- Hygiene (brushing your teeth, washing your body, clipping your nails)

- Daily preparation (packing your bag for work, getting dressed for the day, making lunch)

- Rest (when you wake up for the day, when you go to bed for the night, the way that you go to bed)

Rituals

- Daily (drinking coffee with your partner, getting ready for the day, doing the crossword puzzle together)

- Weekly or monthly (Friday night dates, Sunday check-ins, working out together)

- Annual (your anniversary, special holidays, birthdays)

CHAPTER 7

Manage Your Thirds

A ndrew and I have had a long day at work and we're plopped in front of our TV. It's blasting some sort of daily horror story from the news, but neither of us is paying attention. We're glued to something much more important to us, and it's not our relationship; it's our phone.

We want connection, but we aren't prioritizing getting it from each other because we are getting it everywhere else.

Connection to world news

Connection to strangers on Instagram

Connection to our jobs through the Gmail app

Connection to our friends through iMessage

Connection to the opinions of strangers on X, the social media app formerly known as Twitter

Suddenly, though, I decide I want connection with Andrew. I look up and scoff. "If we are going to sit together, can you at least put your phone away?"

"What? You've been on your phone the entire time. I only picked mine up because you had yours."

I am frustrated because I know he is right. I haven't been managing my phone use well. When I get tired, I just want to scroll. Yet, I know scrolling does nothing for me. Our phone use is a major issue in our relationship. It often feels like another partner in the room whom we have to compete with. And while we both recognize the problem, it's taking effort to eradicate it.

"You're right," I say. "What should we do instead?"

We decide to watch a show together. We put the phones in another room and lay side by side on the couch. We are tired, so we don't need to be talking or partaking in something active. Being together with our shared attention on something is enough.

I feel Andrew's hand wrap around my waist and I grab it and give it a squeeze. We lay there together watching until we both fall asleep.

HOW TO CREATE A SAFE COCOON

While being in a relationship means signing up for a lifetime of stressors with each other, it also means committing to being each other's safe cocoon. Doing this requires you to make decisions regarding how you navigate yourself and the outside world that are beneficial to the unit as a whole.

Stan Tatkin, the founder of Psychobiological Approach to Couples Therapy, coined the term *the couple bubble* to help couples better understand what their boundaries of protection should look like. According to Tatkin, the couple bubble describes the mutually constructed membrane, cocoon, or womb that holds a couple together and protects each partner from outside elements."[1]

Many of the couples I work with pierce the shell of their cocoon with poor boundaries by something Stan Tatkin calls "thirds." Thirds are anything outside of your relationship that might threaten your connection by draining your energy, resources, and trust. This might be hobbies, in-laws, the workplace, substances, or friends, to name a few.

Each time they pierce the shell, it becomes weaker, removing the security of the relationship little by little. Couples might pierce the cocoon by taking the advice and opinions of outsiders over those of their partner, by spending money that wasn't agreed on, by overusing substances, and by choosing to dedicate more time to work than to each other.

Every duo has some thirds. A third between my best friend and I might be my cell phone use when we are out at dinner. A third between my husband and I could be my job.

There are so many threats to our cocoon in modern society that sometimes it's hard to figure out what is causing the actual issue. Week after week, I meet with couples who believe they are failing—they can't keep up with the laundry, they don't have time to plan birthday parties, they haven't had energy for sex—and week after week they try doing things that should help.

- They work on communicating better about what needs to be done.

- They divide the labor more fairly.

- They outsource.

When thirds are being mismanaged, relationships struggle. Managing thirds (and thereby managing stress) means first being able to identify them and the harm they can cause.

Couple Profile

Leann (42/F) and Cora (37/F) have been married for ten years and are living in the suburbs with one child. Leann is a teacher and Cora is a pediatrician. The pandemic was especially hard on them. Cora and Leann have experienced an increased workload and less time at home. The stress of managing it all has increased conflict. They have also noticed unhealthy coping mechanisms, like drinking. They come to therapy to reduce conflict and improve their health.

It's late 2021 and Leann and Cora are telling me how frustrated they are with the number of tasks they have to complete in their daily life—how it all seems unending and how they aren't sure what to do about it.

When couples express to me that they are jointly overwhelmed and not sure exactly what to do to make their daily lives more manageable, I do an activity with them that is inspired by Eve Rodsky's Fair Play system. I rip five sheets of paper out of my notebook and label them one by one:

1. Magic

2. Housework

3. Childcare

4. Work life

5. Unpredictable

I put the sheets side by side on the table between us. "Look at each of these categories together. I want you to write down everything that needs to be done in your family." They both pick up a pen and take a moment to look over the categories. Then, together, they work to fill the sheets of paper.

As Leann and Cora work together on the task, I watch them fill the **unpredictable** category:

- School keeps calling us to pick up Liam because he has the sniffles.

- Every week there seems to be an issue with an appliance in the house.

- When our Wi-Fi isn't strong enough, we have to run to the office.

And the **work life** category:

- I have to submit my hours by Friday at 5:00 pm.

- I need to submit my name change so we can keep our insurance.

- I have to update my license before it lapses.

- My continuing education units are due next week.

And **childcare**:

- Baths

- Teeth

- Books

- Playing

And **housework**:

- Dishes

- Laundry

- Cleaning the guinea pig cage

- . . . and on and on and on and on

And then they got to **magic**.

"What does this one mean?" Leann asks.

"It's the category for the tasks you complete to make sure the special stuff happens in your life," I respond.

Leann and Cora look blankly at each other and then at me. "You know," I say, "picking up each other's favorite bagels on Sunday morning or planting a new bush each year or changing the wreath on the door for the new season . . . the things that make life feel special, fresh, and magic."

Leann immediately starts to cry. "What's going on Leann?" I ask.

"I don't think we have anything magic in our lives right now and it makes me really sad. Liam deserves magic."

"So do you," I say. "You deserve magic too."

Leann and Cora share with me that they don't have any rituals and they haven't had time to do the things they used to do—surprising each other with treats, hanging lights in the winter, setting up a beachy spread on the mantle above the fireplace in the summer. "It used to be something I loved to do," says Leann, "but I feel like neither of us protects that part of our lives."

For Leann and Cora, recognizing that there was no time to make life sparkle made them realize how dull life had become. And this was not the life they had set out to create. Yet even with all of their efforts they felt they couldn't get their heads above water.

No matter how much Cora wanted to hang a wreath, the continuing education units had to be submitted for her medical license first.

No matter how much Leann wanted to take a trip to Dunkin' Donuts to grab Cora's favorite coffee on a Saturday morning, she needed to get her fingerprints notarized first.

No matter how much they both wanted to surprise Liam with a scavenger hunt in the backyard after school, they had to plop him in front of the TV because both of their jobs required after-hours work.

"Our workplaces," I say, "have become the dullest, sharpest knives for many couples. Dull, because they've filled, without limit, our lives with endless mundane tasks. Sharp, because it really hurts to recognize what it's taking away—the things that really matter."

Somehow, we went from couples ending their workday and coming home to eat dinner together to having twenty-four-hour workdays with tiny breaks. Let's take a look at Leann's workday. Leann is a teacher:

- 7:30 am–4:00 pm:

  Teaching (all lesson-planning time has been removed by the school district)

- 4:00 pm–6:30 pm:

  Pick up Liam and "have a break from work" to play with him

- 6:30 pm–7:30 pm:

  Hand off Liam to Cora to spend time lesson planning

- 7:30 pm–8:00 pm:

  Take a break from work to make and eat dinner

- 8:00 pm–8:30 pm:

  Get back to parent emails

- 8:30 pm and beyond:

  Take a break from work to get ready for bed

Let's look at Cora's schedule. Cora is a pediatrician:

- 6:00 am–6:00 pm:

  Meeting with patients (the time for writing required notes has been taken away in order to see more patients)

- 6:00 pm–7:30 pm:

  Drive home and play with Liam

- 7:30 pm–8:00 pm:

  Eat dinner

- 8:00 pm–8:30 pm:

  Put Liam to bed

- 8:30 pm and beyond:

  Finish medical notes and get ready for bed

Leann and Cora are on a twenty-four-hour work cycle, although they are not being paid for it. And, within that work cycle, they have gaslit themselves into believing that the fact they can't quite figure out how to get all of their tasks done and still make things special is an individual or relational failing.

In addition, the tasks that make their careers sparkle are being edged out by tasks that make them darkle (this is a real word by the way; it means to become clouded or gloomy). The teacher who loves to help children build dioramas is now filling out twenty documents a day to report to some data analyst on the school board. The doctor who wants to sit with their patient and understand what is going on, is stuck signing into portals, responding to bad faith insurance denials, and fielding phone calls all day.

Many couples are trying to emulate an old paradigm—come home, eat dinner together, and read a book or watch the news—but they can't because the Slack pings never stop.

INTENTIONAL SACRIFICES

The next time I meet with Leann and Cora, they are much more motivated. "It was really an aha moment for us to realize that we are both so miserable because there just isn't time for magic in our lives. Something about uncovering that helped us stop pointing fingers at each other. It's not Leann's fault that we don't have that. Our lives just aren't allowing time for it. What do we do, Liz?" Cora shares.

"I am not sure of the answer," I tell Leann and Cora. "As a couple, you're going to need to find a creative solution to this because it isn't going to work for you or your family."

Leann says, "Well, I love my job, and I know my boss won't let me change much about it."

And Cora responds with, "Your job will never love you like Liam and I do, though."

"Let's take a pause. I don't think we should jump into solutions too quickly. They won't stick if we do that," I say.

Asking Cora and Leann to take a pause is a popular relationship intervention. When people are stressed and have a dilemma to solve, they tend to quickly jump into solutions. However, the solutions tend not to stick. They don't stick because at least one person agreed to it half-heartedly.

Instead, I encourage couples to take a pause and talk about the issue they are facing; to have some deep conversations around it and really get to know each other on the topic. You can come to solutions after that, but deciding on solutions without comprehending each person's point of view isn't going to work.

"Why don't you ask each other some more questions," I share. "See if you can better understand what is important to each of you."

As Leann and Cora talk, it is clear that the type of life they value is not the type of life they are living. They know something needs to change and recognize there are no easy answers.

"This isn't going to be an overnight fix," I tell them. "This is going to be an intentional, slow process that helps you move toward what you want."

In our fast-paced society, we often want to believe that we should be able to find the answer that will quickly fix things. As a realist, I have found that change takes time. You might not be able to quit your job overnight, but you can begin to take small intentional steps toward the lifestyle changes you need in order for your relationship to thrive.

When these lifestyle changes—and sacrifices—become intentional, you are rebelling against the unhealthy sacrifices being marketed to you. "Society" wants you to think you need to make more money so you can buy more stuff. Your intentional sacrifice might be to make less money to have more time for yourself or your loved ones. Intentional sacrifice means thinking about what matters to you and recognizing that to gain it you will need to deal with some loss.

By this point, Andrew and I had been working together for over a year to figure out how to improve our work-life situation since that day I failed Bria and Andrew was let down by work and we felt we had failed everyone. And I knew there were no easy paths, no clear choices. What we found was that there were just intentional sacrifices. These were the things that we had to give up in order to save our family.

That night, we realized something had to give. Someone needed to lean out. At this point in our careers, Andrew was feeling less fulfilled with his work, and I was feeling more fulfilled in mine. As a therapist working through the pandemic, there was nothing more sacred than the work I was doing sitting alongside my clients as they processed stress, fear, and loss. While stressful and tiring, it was meaningful and necessary work.

My husband, on the other hand, was working for corporate America in the midst of a worldwide trauma that only corporate America would respond to by making people feel even worse—layoffs, fear tactics, longer office hours with less pay, and a lack of time to really connect with colleagues. Andrew's workplace had become like *The Hunger Games*. There were no allies. Everyone was out for themselves.

After many conversations, Andrew and I decided together that he would leave his job. This wasn't settled lightly. It was a hard decision to make because there was so much to unravel:

- What does this mean for Andrew's perception of himself?

- How does this impact his future career trajectory?

- What will others think?

- What type of financial risk are we taking? What happens if we can't live off of one salary?

- Are we both as evolved as we think we are when it comes to traditional gender roles? Will this in any way make me feel less feminine and Andrew feel less masculine?

Andrew and I have had many conversations about the decision. Some of them have resulted in reflecting on the issues that have arisen—I won't paint the picture of my husband leaving his job to support my career as being completely rosy. There are very real implications—the same as if I had left mine. Work is meaningful and changing it can hurt. Gendered self and social perceptions still exist. In fact, a study out of the University of Bath found that when men are not the breadwinner, their mental health suffers.[2] And any woman can identify with the reality that it can be hard to balance our passions outside of the home with what we believe we are responsible for within the home.

We sacrificed a lot—financial cushion, certainty, some goals, and even pieces of our identity. But it was an intentional choice. We were very lucky that we were in a place to make the sacrifices we did. Many people can't take a risk like this, but you don't have to leave a job to find a solution. That's why it's important to go through the steps and exercises I've laid out in this book to find your own way forward.

When I work with couples on what work means to their identity, how it plays a role in their attraction to each other, and what losing it will do to their finances, it's important to make space for both/and.

It might have been the best decision for Andrew to leave his job to care of George while I worked AND it's created challenges for us financially, emotionally, and relationally.

As you navigate how stress plays a role in your own family life and begin to make decisions about what needs to change in order for it to improve, it's important to note that not every change is going to feel completely good. Some will require sacrifice. Some will create sadness, grief, and uncertainty. And, if the net value is greater than the loss, then it still might be the best thing to do.

PROTECTING OUR RELATIONSHIPS

Relationships are protected from harm by boundaries. These boundaries are not just for partners to have with each other, but for couples to have with their thirds. It can be hard to set boundaries. Sometimes it means letting other people down, but it might mean lifting your family up. When stress is hurting our relationships, we need boundaries around the things that are causing that stress.

A few months after our conversation about work boundaries, Cora is sitting on my couch next to Leann. She is fiddling with her hoop earrings, looking at the floor, and kicking her foot up and down as she starts telling me about a current shame spiral she is experiencing. Tears stream down her face as she shares that she had too much to drink the night before and her hangover ruined everyone's morning.

Cora has an issue with drinking. It's been downplayed because their lives are so busy and she is so "functional."

Leann takes a deep breath. I can tell she is frustrated with Cora's drinking but also doesn't want to shame her.

"Cora," I say, "there is a lot to unpack with the drinking, but I think we need to start with having new boundaries around alcohol in your life."

"I am not cutting out alcohol," Cora retorts. "I know, I know, you and Leann can sit there and judge me all you want, but this is the only way I connect with people. It's all I have to unwind."

I take a deep breath and show her that I understand. But Cora doesn't feel understood.

"There is no way you can understand, Liz. I need to have this time with my friends. But of course, you probably never do anything to negatively impact your relationship," she says with more than a hint of sarcasm.

I understand more than you could know, I think.

While I am not struggling with drinking, I have certainly impacted my marriage by not setting good boundaries. My husband purchased us tickets to see his favorite band the previous night, and I had completely forgotten and scheduled a client during the time of the concert. Once I realized my error, I let down my husband rather than letting down my client. I helped my client work through loneliness while my husband went to the show alone.

Cora's voice disrupts my own shame spiral. "I am just so tired of being judged," she says.

Cora and I are having a parallel experience. I hear her—she is afraid to change her relationship with alcohol in the same way I am afraid to change my relationship with boundaries in general. But why is it scarier to change those relationships than it is to protect our most important connections? And while I empathize with Cora, I also know I need to lift Leann up and advocate for her and the impact Cora and her drinking are having on their life.

"I hear you. The thing is, you're risking losing your partner by not look-ing at the impact of alcohol and making some changes," I say. "Each time you drink you are saying yes to alcohol and no to your family. It sucks to have to choose, but in this instance, you're going to have to decide which hardship you want to face—the pain and difficulty of changing your rela-tionship with alcohol or losing your relationship with Leann."

"Yeah, I agree with that," Leann chimes in, "I think you need to stop spending time with your friends at bars. It's not good for you."

Not so fast, I think. Leann enjoys a beer every night. Leann, though, is able to drink one or two and then stop. She doesn't end up hungover. She doesn't send off embarrassing emails to her boss in the middle of the night. Because of her genetics, she isn't predisposed to alcohol abuse the way Cora is.

I smile at Cora and turn to Leann. "You need better boundaries with alcohol too." I continue, "Relationships and their challenges take joint effort. If your partner has a drinking problem, it's time to stop drinking around them and stop bringing tons of alcohol into the house. You're just exacerbating the issue."

Cora and Leann are uncomfortable with what I've said. Leann shares that it would be embarrassing for her to no longer drink at social outings. "Everyone is going to think I am an alcoholic if all of the sudden I order Sprite instead of wine."

And Cora says, "Well now I have no idea who I am going to hang out with. And I feel like shit that Leann is having to change her habits for me."

I let them talk out their discomfort and then I respond.

"The thing about boundaries is that they aren't always easy. Sometimes they really suck. And with the most important boundaries there is often some form of sacrifice. Just because you set a boundary doesn't mean it's going to feel good."

When I coach couples to set boundaries in order to save their most sacred relationships, we talk a lot about what-ifs. I think it's important to explore fears because they're often real. "Leann," I say, "let's play this out . . . you go to a work dinner and your colleagues laugh at you for drinking a Sprite . . . so what happens then?"

"If people laugh at me for drinking a Sprite, I would honestly think they are idiots."

"Okay, so what if they go home and gossip that you must be an alcoholic, then what?"

"If anyone thinks that they must not know me well, so I wouldn't care," she responds.

I play out the what-ifs with both Leann and Cora until they realize that they can handle making the changes they need.

It's not always as easy as that though. The reality might be truly painful. If you're learning to set boundaries with your in-laws, you might get ousted from the family unit. If you set boundaries with your boss, you might lose your job.

Sometimes, there will be a painful outcome when you begin changing the way you navigate life. Instead of avoiding the change, couples need to consider what plans need to be set into place so they can prepare for difficult outcomes.

For example, if you're worried that setting an important boundary at work could cause you to be fired, you might set up some job interviews first . . . just in case. Or, if you have a parent whom you spend a lot of time helping and you're worried it will impact them if you take some of your time back, maybe you come up with a plan for how they can get support outside of you.

SETTING BOUNDARIES WITH EACH OTHER

Having healthy boundaries in a relationship isn't just about what you do with your thirds, it's also what you do with each other. No matter how much you love someone or how close you feel, you need limitations. Boundaries make things clear and reduce stress.

A few months after agreeing to stay away from alcohol, Cora emails me:

> Hey Liz,
>
> Sorry to bother you. Leann brought a bottle of wine home for Thanksgiving. I don't think it's a good idea, but also don't want to seem controlling. Any ideas on what to do?

After reading her email, I sent Cora a brief message asking if she would be willing to hop on a quick telehealth call. She agrees.

During the session, we talk about what is holding her back from setting a boundary with Leann. They had agreed to have no alcohol in the house and it wouldn't be shocking for Cora to ask Leann to remove it.

"I want to be able to be okay with alcohol in the house," Cora shares.

She tucks her hair behind her ears and looks up toward the ceiling and then back at me. "I just feel like I should be able to handle it. My drinking issue shouldn't be her issue."

"You're in a relationship with each other—a family to each other. You committed to reducing the impact of alcohol on your relationship and your health together. It is okay to expect Leann to follow through on that commitment."

Cora is falling into a common trap that makes it difficult to hold limits. She wants to be passive—the type of communication that requires us to be uncomfortable so others don't have to be.

But a supportive relationship requires us to set limits. We cannot absorb the discomfort just to keep the peace. We need to learn to be assertive.

Being assertive means taking accountability for yourself while also giving others the opportunity to take responsibility for themselves.

I coach Cora in how to be assertive with Leann. We work on maintaining a gentle tone of voice, expressing messages that have an underpinning of love, and speaking for herself. "I think I could just gently say to her, 'Leann, I love how great things have been between us without alcohol. I'd like us to stick to our agreement of no alcohol in the house, even on Thanksgiving.'"

"That's great, Cora. That's setting limits with love."

Setting limits with love looks like:

- Using a gentle tone of voice

- Tending to attachment needs to help your partner feel secure in the relationship

- Taking care of yourself

- Avoiding blame, criticism, and force

- Focusing on your own behaviors in the moment

Setting limits with love isn't just useful when discussing how alcohol is managed in your home or how much time is dedicated to work. It can also apply to situations where you have to set a limit regarding your interactions with each other.

When Andrew and I start to utilize our go-tos—criticism and defensiveness—in an argument, we set limits. Since the early days of our relationship, strong boundaries have helped us reduce significant distress. Instead of continuing the conversation or criticizing Andrew when he becomes defensive, I say, "Andrew, I need you to hear me out. I am going to take a break and we can try to talk again in a little bit."

And when I get critical? Andrew responds with something like, "Liz, I want to hear you out and I can't hear you when you're putting me down. I'll listen when you can share it with me in another way."

Doing this creates a safe environment between the two of us—one in which we are less likely to become physiologically dysregulated.

PUTTING IT INTO PRACTICE

The concept of boundaries often makes sense to people. But putting them into practice is another story. That's because when we move from thinking about a boundary to actually setting it, we are required to feel. And often the initial feeling is discomfort, something that most people attempt to avoid at all costs.

It's one thing to know that you have to tell your boss that leaving the office at 8:00 pm is no longer appropriate, but it's another thing to actually do it and to experience the emotions that come with it.

I attended an event with the Female Founders Fund called Agents of Change. At this event, Rashida Jones, the president of MSNBC, was being interviewed about her experience as a woman in business. "You're a leader and people say it's lonely at the top," the interviewer said. "Do you have tips on how to deal with that loneliness?"

Most of the presenters had offered tips like, "Make sure you pick a great board so that you know you've got people on your side," or "Surround yourself with other powerful women." But when Jones was asked this question, she paused. She took a moment to look around the room and then smiled at the audience. "You know, my biggest advice is that you still maintain a life outside of this. That you don't only iden- tify as a leader. I have some leadership peers who I go to, yes, but more importantly I have things I do beyond this role. I have boundaries with this role."

She went on to share that setting boundaries is hard because you worry you might let people down, but that often when she steps away and does the other things she needs to do in life, she feels much better. "I will never complete the entire list. I put it away at a certain point and then I go spend time with my kids. I had to stop yesterday because I promised my daughter I'd be at her game. And guess where I was at 5:15 pm? Her game."

Jones was exemplifying what it means to recognize when something is difficult and to do it anyway because ultimately it will be good for you (and your family) in the long run.

People tend to avoid setting limits, even if those limits are good for them and their family, for two reasons:

- They don't have the words to set the boundary.

- Setting the limit makes them feel something that they believe they can't cope with.

After Leann and Cora realized how much magic was missing in their lives and how much alcohol was impacting their happiness, they felt committed to setting more limits and making difficult choices that would help them change their lifestyle. As they started to reduce the outside stressors in their lives, they began arguing less and therefore coming to therapy less.

During one of our monthly appointments, I ask them how things are going.

Cora shares, "It's pretty great. I've been really working to complete what I can complete during the workday and if the other stuff doesn't get done, then I add it to a list to bring up to my supervisor later. If they want to assign me more work than is humanly possible to complete, then that's on them."

I smile at Cora and turn to Leann.

"I guess it's going well. Cora has worked really hard on changing things. I, on the other hand, have really struggled to make some changes I know I need to make."

"Like what?" I ask, encouraging her to share more.

Leann is a helper at heart. She cares deeply about the students and their families. She is motivated by "doing the right thing." It makes sense she is having a hard time setting limits.

"I really want to have undisrupted time with my family at night, but if one of the kids is struggling at school, then I always make time for them or their parents in the evening to chat about what's going on. And it's not a one-off . . . it's like every night."

Oof. I relate. As do most people in helping professions. It is hard to tell someone you aren't available when they are struggling. But there is no benefit if saying yes is putting the helper into deeper and deeper burnout.

"Leann, what's blocking you from protecting that time?"

She looks uncomfortable, frustrated even. "I don't know what I am even supposed to say. Plus I see all these TikTok videos and Twitter videos criticizing the shit out of teachers for not caring. Last night, a parent was complaining about a teacher who wouldn't return their calls at night. So I just feel like such a bad person if I say no."

"Ah, okay," I nod my head. "So one blocker is that you don't know what to say. You need a script or something. And the other blocker is that it's going to feel really uncomfortable."

Leann agrees with my assessment and so I help her. She needs to know the basics. First, what does it sound like to set a boundary? When setting a boundary, you have to decide if you want to say a flat-out "no," "yes" with a caveat, or offer an alternate suggestion to the request. I share some examples with her:

1. When you want to say no

    If your response to a request or to something someone has done is a no, then work toward responding in a brief and neutral tone. For example, "Hi John, I won't be able to stay until 8:00 pm tonight. I will see you tomorrow!"

2. When you want to say yes, but with a limit

    Perhaps you've been given a request that you can accept to a point. Maybe you'd like to have your mother-in-law at the hospital during the birth of your baby, but you'd like to be with your partner most of the time. This situation calls for saying yes and setting a limit. For example, "Absolutely! We would love you to be at the hospital while baby number two is born! It's really important we get some family time, so we will have visiting hours for the first hour after the birth."

3. When you want to offer an alternative

    At times we are asked something that we want to say no to, but we have another idea of how we can fulfill the request or need. Consider being invited to an event with friends. Perhaps the weekend isn't going to work because you promised your partner you'd go on a date. In this case, you can say, "I can't go this weekend, but could go next weekend. Is anyone available then?"

These examples help Leann to see that setting a limit can come with flexibility. It doesn't need to be harsh.

"Okay, this helps," she says. "So what do I do about my anxiety for being judged?"

For Leann, in order to make important changes, she has to accept what is—she cannot please the parents and administration at her school 100 percent of the time while still being there for her family. The other reality she needs to accept is that she will likely have feelings about that. She shares that she thinks she will feel guilt and embarrassment. Potentially even shame.

Once Leann accepted the reality, she could plan for how to best deal with those uncomfortable feelings. For her, it was letting Cora know how she was feeling whenever she had to let a parent down.

When I ask her later how she started dealing with parents asking for evening phone calls, she shared that her response would sound something like this:

> Dear parent,
>
> I would love to connect with you about your child's grades. I can't do evening phone calls, but I am free tomorrow during my 11:00 am prep period. Would that work for you?

Leann was setting a limit around her evening hours while also offering an alternative. Of course, this brought along with it the issue of not having enough time to prepare, but Leann put the problem on a list to bring up with her boss. Just like Cora, she realized that if her work can't get done during the time she's meant to be at work, then it is a bigger systemic issue to solve—not hers to figure out on her own.

SESSION NOTES:

In this session, we explored thirds. You learned what thirds are and how they can impact the energy we are able to offer the people we love the most. We explored techniques you can use to navigate thirds like name it to tame it, nonviolent communication, boundaries, and limits.

By using these techniques you'll protect your relationship and preserve its energy.

1. INTERVENTION: NAMING YOUR THIRDS

List all of the thirds in your life (hint: there might be a lot!). Then, rate them based on how much of an impact they have on your relationship . . . 1 has the lowest impact and a 5 has the highest impact.

2. INTERVENTION: NAME IT TO TAME IT

Name it to tame it is a science-backed tool created by Daniel Siegel that helps you notice and label your emotions. It can help calm spiraling thoughts and soothe emotions resulting from stress, emotions like rage, anxiety, and fear.

When you catch yourself spiraling, name the feeling. For example, if you notice yourself becoming stressed and overwhelmed, close your eyes, put your hand on your chest, and name the emotion: "I am feeling really stressed right now." This act alone helps to reduce stress and soothe difficult feelings.

3. INTERVENTION: IDENTIFYING TASKS

Identifying tasks is a great way to get a clear picture of where each of your stressors is coming from . . . and where you're neglecting yourself and your partner.

Rip out five sheets of paper and write one category on each:

1. Magic

2. Housework

3. Childcare

4. Work Life

5. Unpredictable

Take time with your partner to fill out everything you have to do in each category. Then, label each activity with who tends to be responsible for it.

4. INTERVENTION: BOUNDARIES

Think of one or two boundaries you want to set with your partner. Perhaps they utilize defensiveness, stay at work too late, don't pick up their socks, or get critical. Write a note to yourself about what you want to say when it happens and how you want to respond. For example, if your partner spends too much time and energy playing video games, you might say, "I am going to bed at 9:00 pm each night, so if you play for a long time, we will end up missing time together."

5. INTERVENTION: LIMIT SETTING

When you need to set a limit, decide if you want to say no, yes with a limit, or offer an alternative. For example, if your colleague asks you to help them on a project but you know it is going to take away from important family time, you can respond in a few ways:

- No: "I am unable to help with that this week."

- Yes, with a limit: "Sure, I can help! I will have fifteen minutes after lunch."

- Offer an alternative: "I am not able to help this week but I can help next week."

CHAPTER 8

Accept Reality

Allie and I have been standing in the checkout line at our favorite big box store together for about ten minutes. She's frustrated because the store said they would hold something for her and they didn't.

"I came back when you told me to," she says in a calm voice. "Do you know what happened?"

"Couldn't tell ya," the cashier responds as they walk away. Allie understands people are human, but she's a little miffed by the fact that they didn't even apologize for the inconvenience. I'm listening to her talk about it as I feel my phone vibrate. I pick it up and notice it's a text from my husband.

"Dunno why the hell these companies think they are entitled to waste our time. I've been on the phone with the credit card company again dealing with this dispute for forty-five minutes," the text says.

Me neither, I think.

"What is going on with the way businesses treat their customers?" I turn to ask Allie. I tell her about the text I just got and what has happened to my husband and I over the last year. In April, we purchased a swing set for my son. It took years of saving before we finally felt comfortable enough to spend the money—$4,899 to be exact.

But the set never arrived—only a swing did.

We received an endless barrage of "your order is experiencing delays" emails. When we tried to call, we were sent from representative to representative since none of them could help us and all of them thought they knew who could.

After trying for months to get a refund, we filed a dispute with the credit card company. We didn't take it lightly, but it seemed like the only way to get our money back.

The place we ordered the swing set from, however, sent the picture of the itty-bitty swing box to legitimize that they had sent a $4,899 swing set. And the credit card company agreed with them.

It's October now. We have no swing set. The credit card company refused the chargeback, and the store still won't give us our money back (they finally sent a check, but for the wrong amount). We've spent hundreds of hours disputing the issue. And, my husband and I have gotten in disputes with each other over the damn dispute.

Allie laughed. "Oh, well have I got a story for you!" She went on to tell me about how she bought something from a phone company in the store. Like most things these days, it broke immediately. She brought it back to find that while the store could sell it to her, they weren't "authorized" to provide refunds. She would need to go home and call another company to get that worked out. So she did and they sent her a new one. But the new one didn't work either. "I know it sounds stupid," Allie says. "But it's made me so enraged, and I have been snappy with John and the kids."

She continued to share that she went back to the store and begged them for help. "I've spent hours on the phone dealing with this. Please just help me with the return." Finally, they agreed. They sold her a replacement item in the store and told her they would send a return box. Once she made the return, she would get a refund.

But the return box never came and neither did her refund.

Anytime I bring up the issue we had with the swing set to my friends, I hear story after story of similar experiences. Companies selling items that never come or are defective or services that are never given. In order to request a refund, people are sent through a rigmarole that never results in anything but lost money, time, and sanity.

This year alone, my husband has wasted countless hours dealing with our internet provider, who wasn't providing the internet speed we paid for, the store that never sent the swing set, and our insurance company, who seemingly always processes the claim the wrong way on "accident."

Overworked and underpaid representatives and shoddy technology are being made responsible for business policies. Both get the blame ("Why is that agent so rude?!" or "Sorry! Our system won't let me issue the refund. It doesn't work that way!"), but really, out-of-control greed is fueling the problem.

Companies like the swing set store keep our money and make record sales.

Some of this might occur because of poor systems, but it can't all be explained away in that manner. Companies know that the overburdened and battered American public just won't be able to keep going and at some point, will give up, allowing the company to keep their money with little to no recourse for the average person.

My husband and I both respond to this truth with justified anger. We feel gaslit and taken advantage of, and we don't know what else to do. We've spent many nights arguing with each other as a reaction to these issues. And if we aren't careful, we get stuck in our stress cycles and can't get out.

RADICAL ACCEPTANCE

When my husband and I faced the swing set issue, we felt stress for a number of reasons—the amount of money it cost, the time it took to figure it out, and our differing opinions on the issue. But when I think about what caused conflict between the two of us, it comes down to our rigid beliefs about what is or isn't fair.

Couples commonly get caught up in the stress of navigating fairness between each other or the outside world. They get stuck when they keep repeating to themselves and each other things like:

"This isn't fair!"

"I don't know why this is happening to me!"

"I'll take a step when they take a step."

In an interview between Lady Gaga and Oprah, Oprah shared, "All stress comes from wanting something to be what it isn't. And it doesn't change until you first accept it for what it is, and then make a decision about what to do next."[1]

We can't totally avoid hardship, so when we face it, we have to be willing to look it in the eye. There is no magic pill that will protect you from pain, discomfort, and stress. It brings to mind a quote by Haruki Murakami, "Pain is inevitable. Suffering is optional."[2]

Quite frankly, a partner who constantly gets stuck in what is fair and what isn't fair becomes, at the very least, annoying to their partner, and at the very worst, an impediment. Too much energy is wasted on trying to prove a point and blame.

Being stuck in this cycle creates a system where someone else has to accept the reality and then take responsibility for it.

We can validate that something isn't fair—it's absolutely unfair, unethical, and horrible that people cannot get business done with large companies without feeling completely taken advantage of—but each of us still must take accountability within our own lives for the next step we make.

You get four choices in an unfair situation:

- Continue your denial and therefore your misery.

- Allow it to be.

- Try to change it.

- Try to distance yourself from it or quit it.

Choosing the last three options is difficult. When people in relationships avoid doing the hard thing that's needed to make their lives and relationships better, it's often about the illusion of control. The idea is that if we can teach the jerk a lesson or do all of the things to please our partners, bosses, kids, and friends, then we'll be able to control our own bad feelings in such a way that we feel happy.

Instead of staying stuck, radical acceptance requires us to move from a willful stance ("I need to teach them a lesson") to a willing stance ("I am willing to make a choice that helps me feel better"). With a willing stance you don't fight with what is. You don't let your emotions run you. You accept the reality, even if you don't condone it.

Whenever I first introduce radical acceptance to clients, they hear it as "radical approval." It is not the same thing. Accepting doesn't mean you approve. It means you are able to look at reality, accept that it is there, and take steps to live within that reality.

> When you accept that you and your partner are in debt, you can begin to live within your means.

> When you accept that you have experienced a significant loss, you can begin to grieve.

> When you accept that you do not have what others have, you can figure out how to live with what you've got.

Radical acceptance is a concept that was introduced by Marsha Linehan in her treatment approach known as dialectical behavior therapy, which was initially created to help individuals manage emotions and relationships in a healthier way.[3] However, I use the concept of radical acceptance with couples because it helps them move their focus away from thoughts and actions that are unproductive and allows for them to use their energy in a more helpful manner.

By radically accepting the truth of our lives, we allow our mind, emotions, and body to lean into the reality that we cannot change what is. By doing this, we release ourselves from the traps of resentment and bitterness and can begin to take control of our lives. And, if there is no control to be taken, we can begin to learn to cope with the life we have.

The greatest paradox is that to change something you don't like, you must first accept it.

Couple Profile

Leslie (27/F) and Mei (26/F) have been together for five years. They have what they describe as a happy relationship; however, they also experience a lot of stress within their individual lives. They have busy jobs and have struggled with a string of illnesses. They come to therapy to learn best practices for a healthy relationship.

Leslie is animated as she steps into my office with Mei by her side. Smiling ear to ear, she holds her hand up to show me the shining ruby on her left ring finger. "We're engaged," she gushes.

During our session, Leslie and Mei share the details of their engagement. Mei proposed to Leslie at their favorite beach location, and all of their friends and family were there to celebrate. They spent time reflecting on how far they'd come as a couple.

When I first met with Leslie and Mei they were absolutely buried beneath a pile of stress. Leslie was navigating a chronic illness and a new job while Mei was navigating a complex relationship with her aging parents. While they didn't argue much, they also didn't connect. Leslie and Mei tended to respond to stress by making themselves busier, burning out, and becoming completely numb and withdrawn. Over the last several months, they had learned how to regulate their stressors in a new way, and it had made all of the difference to their relationship.

Now, they only come to see me every several weeks for maintenance. Today, they report that while they are certainly excited for their wedding, it is also creating some tension within their relationship. "That makes sense," I share. "Transitions are stressful—even happy ones. Do you notice a pattern in regard to what exactly is causing you stress in your wedding planning?"

"Well, I am the one doing everything," Leslie says. "It makes me feel like Mei just doesn't care and it worries me for the future. What am I getting into? Am I going to have to always deal with the decision-making?"

I've known Mei and Leslie long enough to know that Mei absolutely cares about her wedding. That she loves Leslie and is excited for their next step together. So I was curious why she wasn't being more involved. "Mei, are you disinterested in wedding planning?"

"It's all a headache," Mei says.

Ah, okay, I think. This is on-brand for Mei. When Mei experiences stress, she becomes indignant and shuts down like the opossum.

"So it's been a real pain in the ass already?" I ask.

"Yeah. It's just a racket. We find someone we want to work with in our budget and contact them and then they jack up their rate with hidden fees. We want an outdoor wedding, but then there is all this stuff you need to deal with just to have it in your own backyard. I have to pay for permits for noise, parking, and food. I'm not into playing these games."

As Mei talks, Leslie starts to glaze over. After holding her breath for a few moments she lets out a loud sigh as she picks at the lint on her pants and checks on her painted nails.

"What's going on, Leslie?"

"Oh nothing. I mean, I don't really care at this point if it overwhelms Mei. It sucks she doesn't want to be involved, but it is what it is. I guess I just have to deal with annoying decisions and that is going to be my lot in life."

"Let's not go into this all-or-nothing thinking. I don't want you to crumble into this dynamic every time you face something frustrating. We have an opportunity to deal with this differently," I say.

Leslie and Mei are running into a common pattern in relationships where one partner senses that the other partner isn't able to handle stress of some sort. In order to avoid dealing with the arguments, shut down, and frustrations that ensue, the partner who can "manage it" takes over.

In doing this, they work hard and quietly to make sure everything works and fits just so in order to reduce their partner's sensitivity to frustration. Then, once they've figured it all out, "Voila!" they unveil the outcome . . . only to learn that their partner is unhappy about it.

Throughout my marriage, I've had many similar experiences. Like the time our HOA kept moving a major project from one date to another. The project was a big one and was going to affect the use of our home and create financial impact. Rather than loop my husband into their frustrating attempts at scheduling, I tried to take care of it on my own. I believed my husband would get more worked up than I was if he knew how truly unreasonable they were being. And I believed I could handle the stress better.

Ultimately, though, I had to share with him what was actually going on. He was upset that I had kept him in the dark because it didn't provide him with the opportunity to help solve the problem.

Instead of trying to regulate stress for my husband, I needed to learn that it's my job to regulate myself and that he deserves to know the inner workings of our lives. He needed to learn to recognize and take accountability for his own reactions to stress so that I could feel comfortable sharing. This type of teamwork protects the relationship from bigger issues like betrayal, secrecy, and resentment.

Partners who take on the world together need to recognize it's each person's responsibility to become better stress managers. It's not right for one person to take it all on because the other person becomes wind, flood, or fire anytime something uncomfortable crops up.

Part of improving our relationship with stress is to evaluate our own personal entitlements. In partnerships where one person tends to quietly take on the stress, there is often a difference in belief system. The partner who deals with the stress head-on responds to life's discomforts with, "Oof. Here we go again. This is frustrating and I have to deal with it. Comfort isn't promised to me."

This doesn't mean that this partner enjoys the experience. It doesn't mean that they don't worry or grieve or feel frustrated too. It means they have accepted the reality of their life and are trying to manage it.

Meanwhile, the partner who becomes enraged when things don't go according to plan or puts their head in the sand tends to think and say things like, "Well, I am not going to deal with that because it's not how it's supposed to be. I shouldn't have to feel frustrated, uncomfortable, or do anything I don't want to do."

These people tend to believe they live in Lake Wobegon—a world where they are the special ones, the ones who shouldn't be inconvenienced or distressed or face hardship.

However, none of us are immune to the real world. And the sooner we can accept that and drop our entitlements, the sooner we can work alongside the people we love to actually solve problems and move forward.

The issue that is cropping up for Leslie and Mei is that Mei doesn't believe she should be inconvenienced—by permits, by costs, by timelines. She doesn't believe planning a wedding should be hard. Those are completely fine beliefs, and in fact, I join her in all of them. And yet her beliefs cannot deny reality.

- If they want a backyard wedding, they do need permits.

- If they want the photographer they've been following, they need to pay the rate.

- If they want to plan a wedding, they need to deal with some of the frustrations of it.

"Mei, can I reflect on something I am noticing?"

"Sure," she responds with the openness that she regularly gives.

"I've noticed that when something frustrating happens, your belief that it shouldn't happen trumps the reality that it is actually happening. Have you ever noticed that? Or heard anyone else give you that feedback before?"

"Well, I'm just not a pushover."

"Interesting. Because what I see is that your responses don't get you what you want at all. You might respond in a kind of grandiose way, suggesting that no one is the boss of you, but you never actually get the resolution you want. You just write off the issue."

"It always works out, right?"

"Yes, because Leslie works it out." Ouch. The hard part about being a good couples therapist is that every now and then you have to say something a little bit scathing while also using a likable tone. Otherwise you're a liar or an asshole.

Mei takes a deep breath. I can tell what I just said has rattled her, but she needs to hear the truth. If Leslie and Mei are going to have a long and happy marriage, it can't start with Leslie being the default stress manager. Mei needs to learn to look reality straight in the eye and accept it.

I let what I said sink in for a moment before continuing. "Mei, I have to be honest. I almost always agree with your stances. I too think it is ridiculous to have to get a permit for your own private property. It's not that your stance is wrong; it's that your stance isn't the current reality. If you want things to change, you'll need to run a petition. But even that takes action."

"I hear you," Mei says, looking at the floor as she nods her head. "I do tend to get indignant. I know that. I just can't stand how everything always has to be so hard these days."

I laugh. "It's ridiculous. Truly. Prices are outlandish. The amount of time we waste on the phone with bureaucratic call centers should be a crime. But it's our reality right now. And while you can certainly fight it, you also need to be engaged in your day-to-day life so you can move forward together. So I will ask again, do you care about this wedding?"

"Of course."

"Okay, so instead of shutting down the problem-solving, you need to talk with Leslie about what the reality is and explore next steps. I want you to try that right now. Take a role here."

From there, Mei and Leslie spend the rest of the session talking about the tasks of planning a wedding, their budget, and next steps that needed to be taken. Once Mei realizes that the roadblocks are the reality and not something she can wish away, she is able to take the reins. Mei's acceptance of the reality gives Leslie more space to talk about it.

YOU CAN DO IT

Sometimes people shut down when faced with stressful experiences because they don't believe in themselves. They worry that they aren't resourceful enough to find a solution or that if something bad happens, they won't be able to handle the fallout.

From the Buddhist perspective, a stressful situation is a challenge to believe in yourself like never before. While we don't have to like upsetting events, we can look at them as opportunities for growth and pride. In fact, Hans Selye called stress "the spice of life."[4]

Our suffering, our propensity to blame and pick fights, and our inability to move forward in life are often the result of avoiding the facts of life. Of us not wanting to believe that it's true that we suffer—that things don't work out, that we can't have everything we want, that even with our best efforts, sometimes life will really suck.

We avoid these truths by believing the bad stuff can only happen because there is someone to blame, or by looking for a way to numb the bad stuff by spending more money, using substances, or partaking in anything that allows us to step away from our real life. Because of this, we don't make the hard decisions we need to make in order to get where we want to go. We don't build the relationships we desire and we end up miserable over the idea that misery exists.

MAKING HARD DECISIONS

It is 1:00 am on Saturday morning, and I am sitting on the bed in our guest room with drowsy eyes, a racing heart, and a heavy chest. I think it's anxiety, but it could also be the fact that I am just getting over aspiration pneumonia from how much I've been vomiting the past few weeks. I am four months pregnant with my second child and contending with endless nausea and vomiting that was just recently reduced by the magic drug Zofran.

Three hours ago, I was coaxing my son to bed. As I reminded him that it's healthy to go to bed at a reasonable hour—which would have been three hours before the coaxing began—he told me I was "Out of my mind."

And well, yes, I am out of my mind. But not in the way he meant. He explained that I was absolutely out of my mind to think he should go to bed when he really, really needed to continue practicing his drawings of The Land Before Time characters. "I can't quit, Mom! I need to draw Little Foot."

So, I let him climb into bed and draw Little Foot until he fell asleep on top of his crayons and paper. Then I went to the guest room where I scrolled on Twitter for no less than an hour to get out of my own mind.

As I doomscrolled, I couldn't keep my mind off what was really bothering me. The fact that on Monday—tomorrow—I was going to need to have a very serious talk with some colleagues. And, I knew that they weren't going to like what I had to say.

Like my five-year-old, who was kept awake by the need to continue practicing the outlines of his characters, I lay in bed staring at the blue light of my phone rehearsing in my head what I might say if I say the thing halfway and what I might say if I say the thing all the way. I'm so overwhelmed that even when I am having the conversation in my own mind, the words don't come out. But I do know if I say the thing all the way, the thing I am going to say is that I am quitting one of the many projects I've taken on.

The problem is that I never quit anything. That's a lie—I do quit things like eating healthy, going to the gym, and keeping up with my laundry. But I don't quit relationships or jobs or projects. I just hope that they quit me.

The day before, I went to my first appointment with a new therapist. I parallel parked in front of a brick row house with a swing board sign that read, "Dr. Maura McKenna—Psychologist." Usually I choose therapists based on who seems the floofiest, a word that means mushy and sweet and more embodied than I. But this time, I didn't want the coddling that comes along with it. I wanted tough love. And Dr. McKenna's profile seemed to fit the bill.

I needed to be scared straight. I needed someone to tell me that my life was out of control, that I had too much on my plate. I wanted them to provide me with marching orders, a list, perhaps, with all of the things I should do to get my life in order. Even further, I wanted a script for my Monday conversation.

I walked into Dr. McKenna's office. It didn't look as scary as I had hoped. A fire was burning and there were cozy couches everywhere. I was already being coddled.

I sat down and looked down at my jeans. I had put them on because it felt like a special occasion. Plus, I didn't want her to write in my mental status exam that I looked disheveled. But there it was. Some sort of brown stain. Maybe chocolate? I did, however, have makeup on, so I think that saved me from any low marks in that arena.

"Have you been to therapy before?" Dr. McKenna asked.

"I'm a therapist actually." As soon as I said this, I regretted it. I knew what it could do to tell another therapist that you are a therapist. Sometimes they might stop giving it to you straight. They might say things like, "I'm sure you already know why you do that, so we don't need to go into it," or "You're a therapist, so you understand what's happening here." But I don't. I can see the patterns in others, but not always in myself.

I predicted correctly. Dr. McKenna said, "Oh, okay. Well then there probably won't be a lot I can tell you."

"Oh, well I'm not sure about that. I hope you can help me."

"Why are you here?" she asked.

"I am totally and completely burnt-out," I shared. "It's been a hard year."

I, along with many others, have been feeling the impact of burnout since 2020 and have been constantly swamped by emotional, physical, and mental stress.

I spent a good part of the remaining hour giving her the rundown.

I share that since my husband has taken over at home, I've been able to take on more opportunities. Now, I work multiple jobs at sixty hours a week. But, I also want to offer my presence as a stay-at-home mom, so when my son isn't at school, I do the rest of my work after he goes to bed. I let her know that I never get a break from people. I love people, I tell her, but I am never truly left alone. Emails, direct messages, Slack messages, and texts roll in anytime I step away. I run to the bathroom and come back to several messages asking, "Can you talk?"

"People are always mad," I share. "Probably not more mad than usual—or maybe so, because I think the pandemic has made everyone more irritable. But I have so many people in my orbit that every day I am dealing with at least one person who is unhappy with a decision I have made or the way I've communicated something."

I talk about how hard it is to navigate so many difficult conversations. That I never have a sense of peace.

I share with her that Sam died in September. I cry to her because I haven't really had anyone else to cry to about it. Everyone else was more deserving of the upset, so I let them have it. "That's how it seems to go for me in general," I say. "Everyone else seems more deserving of the upset, so I don't really have anyone to talk to about my own feelings."

Lastly, I explain that my body has been through the ringer. I was hospitalized after getting COVID-19. I had a miscarriage. I am pregnant now, though, and I've had hyperemesis gravidarum.

"What's that?" she asks.

"Oh, it's when you're vomiting upward of ten times a day from pregnancy."

I top it off by sharing that I've just gotten over pneumonia.

I stop. I feel awkward. I have shared too much. I know exactly what she is thinking. She's thinking I am manic or I don't have boundaries or that I've done all of this to myself.

Usually when you say, "I know exactly what they are thinking," you then find out that your assumption was wrong. That the person had a different assessment and it wasn't nearly as critical as you expected.

Not this time. Dr. McKenna responds to everything I shared with an air of judgment. "Well, it sounds like you don't have boundaries, and you need to take something off your plate," she says.

I feel a bit surprised by the lack of empathy. This, though, was the tough love I had set myself up for.

"You're right," I say.

I describe how I wanted to quit the project, but I didn't know how. That I also wanted to make sure I wasn't doing it from a place of reactivity.

Dr. McKenna looks at the clock and lets me know it is time to go.

I leave the session feeling disappointed. I am glad for the tough love, but had been hoping to get some advice. How exactly could I quit the project? I felt so frozen that I wasn't even sure which words I would say. I wanted my marching orders.

And yet, it wasn't on Dr. McKenna to tell me what to do next because I already knew what I needed to do. I needed to take responsibility for my own life. I needed to do the hard thing even though it was uncomfortable.

No matter how much I thought about it, meditated on it, or tried to soothe my feelings around it, the truth was that in order to improve my life, I was going to need to take responsibility for it. It would require me to feel a little yucky at first, but I had to remember that over time it would ultimately help me feel better by significantly reducing the stress in my life.

I needed to have the hard conversation, and no script was going to be the magic pill that made everyone feel good about it. I needed to grieve the loss of the fantasy that I could manage it all, and I would need to learn how to stop running from myself through constant activity.

I ultimately took that responsibility by leaving what I knew no longer served me. And it wasn't fun. It included burned bridges that I could not prevent, guilt, and at times, second-guessing myself.

However, the ultimate outcome was what I needed.

TAKING RESPONSIBILITY

No one wants to feel loss, or sometimes worse, regret. But remembering that when we take responsibility for our lives, while nothing is promised, we become empowered.

Once we notice there is a problem that's causing us distress, it's important to take personal and relational responsibility to make a change.

People struggle to take radical responsibility in many areas—their relationships will be awful because they drink too much but refuse to get help; their bandwidth for connection will be nonexistent because they do far too much for their kids and won't reduce the load.

Learning to do the things that are hard for long-term gain is an important, although sometimes unpleasant, part of creating the life you want. While you can't take responsibility for things you aren't responsible for—and many of our stressors are related to those things—you can take responsibility for your response by setting boundaries, asking for help, self-soothing, or making a decision.

Radical responsibility is about finding choices within even the most difficult situations, and making empowering choices instead of disempowering choices. You always have choices, even if they aren't your preference.

SESSION NOTES:

In this session, we discussed the importance of radical acceptance and responsibility. Even when life is unfair, you will have better outcomes when you face your issues directly instead of spending energy on blame or putting your head in the sand. By using the interventions below, you will learn how to take responsibility and move forward in your life.

1. INTERVENTION: RADICAL ACCEPTANCE

Radical acceptance helps us use our resources wisely when we face unfair or painful experiences in life. If you and your partner are feeling overwhelmed by stress, you can practice radical acceptance. To do this:

- Observe the truth. For example, perhaps you find yourselves stressed every month when you try to pay off the credit card bill. Denial would allow you to avoid looking at the bill or making any changes. Radical acceptance would ask you to look at the bill, recognize that it has become unaffordable, and accept that changes will need to be made on how the credit card is utilized.

- Accept yourself and your partner. This means that you accept how your body, feelings, and thoughts are responding to the issue. For example, using self-compassion or getting more sleep. By accepting your reaction, you can respond to it in a healthy manner.

- Practice opposite action. When individuals face stress, they tend to have a go-to method for reacting to it. Some people avoid and some become reactive. Neither of these methods tends to be helpful long term. Opposite action is doing the opposite of what you usually feel the urge to do. If you tend to ignore the credit card bill until you start getting calls from collections, try reviewing it each day of the week for a little while. If you tend to obsess over the bill, create a structure where you only look at it once a week.

2. INTERVENTION: RADICAL RESPONSIBILITY

Radical responsibility is not about self-blame or blaming your partner; it's about scanning for choices and making the most empowering one. Talk to your partner about a stressor you are facing and make a list of choices that allow you both to take responsibility. When doing this exercise, you can stretch yourself by including outlandish or silly choices to help you come up with options. Then, agree on which responsibility you will each take to change your situation.

CHAPTER 9

Follow a System

My professor is standing in front of class sharing with us how he works with parents who have particularly difficult teenagers. It went something like this: "The problem is," he shares, "that these parents come to me and they are focused on trying to change and control everything. Every behavior is a bad behavior and every behavior gets a reaction. There is no priority on what matters.

"The kid comes home and drops their book bag on the floor instead of hanging it up. What does the parent do? They start to yell, 'Why do you leave the bag that way? Why do you have no respect?'"

He continues, "But the next night, the kid sneaks out of the house. They get drunk at a party. The police come and their parents need to go to the station. The kid gets the same reaction as before, 'Why did you do something so stupid? Why do you have no respect?'

"Both issues receive the same escalatory response. Yet, we know that only one actually deserves this energy. The safety issue is where we really need to work to change things; the book bag just doesn't matter at that moment."

Uri Weinblatt was my professor in graduate school while I was in the family therapy track. He, alongside Haim Omer, created the nonviolent resistance model to help parents navigate acute behavior issues. The premise, at its core, is to help parents deal effectively with their helplessness and isolation, and to control escalatory interactions with their children by helping them prioritize where their energy goes.[1]

To help parents prioritize their energy output, Weinblatt asks them to imagine three different-sized baskets. The largest basket is where everything that doesn't really matter, even if it ticks off the parent, goes. Everything in this basket should be ignored so as to not waste energy or risk connection. This basket should have the most items in it. The medium-sized basket holds items that should be negotiated, and the smallest basket is for one or two issues that the parent recognizes as a priority that need to be actively addressed.

After graduating, I worked with the parents of children who were struggling to regulate their own emotions and behaviors, most often due to trauma. By utilizing the nonviolent resistance model, I was helping them learn how to recognize that their own reactions to stressful family dynamics were only escalating the issues.

From there, I became more focused on my work with adult partners in general. Over time, I saw that not only were adults reacting to their children's behaviors through a cycle of helplessness, isolation, and escalation, but they were reacting to each other in this way too.

As I began to focus more and more of my work on helping couples recognize and change their relationship with stress, I began to adapt the three baskets I used with parents to three baskets couples could use to navigate their lives.

I ask couples to imagine three baskets:

1. Shedding

2. Preventing

3. Adapting

When they use this system together, they can begin to look at their stress in a new way, get a handle on it, and build a more stress-free (or at least, stress-managed) life. Through this chapter, I am going to help you identify what goes in your baskets and how you can continue to explore the baskets over time.

THE WEEKLY MEETING

Couples who feel the most connected and least overwhelmed schedule time to talk. They think about their relationship like a business and have structured time to take care of important matters.

To get started on creating a less stressful life, schedule a meeting that you will commit to every week.

I suggest that couples pick the most realistic time for them. For people who work a nine-to-five job and have kids, usually the evening doesn't work. You're tired, and even if you have the meeting, you'll likely be unprepared and half-hearted. Waking up early on a Sunday or doing it after the kids go to bed Saturday night might be best. Couples who work non-traditional hours might find that lunchtime on Wednesday is best. Consider what truly aligns with your energy levels and availability. An ideal amount of time would be one hour; however, even twenty minutes is better than nothing for the time-crunched couple.

Your meeting should follow the same agenda every single week. This ensures that you don't avoid important topics or get sidetracked. It also will help both of you prepare yourselves for what you'd like to bring up. Here is the agenda I recommend, but I encourage you to make it your own.

1. **Share what you appreciated about your partner during the week.** Be very clear about all the ways in which they helped to make your lives better. A good formula for this is to share what you appreciated, what you noticed about their efforts, how it impacted you, and how it relates to their character overall. For example, "I really appreciated how you dealt with the frustrating exchange with our HOA. You were so on top of it and calm and consistent. It was impressive. Because you owned it, I was able to focus on my work project. I love how you're always able to come up against the most ridiculous things with so much grace."

2. **Share what you think went well for the relationship.** Talk to your partner about the things that went well for your relationship. Whether it was spending more quality time together, tackling a difficult task, or being more patient with each other.

3. **Give feedback on where things could have been better.**
   Without criticism, talk together about what could have
   been better over the past week. Rather than say, "You
   didn't pay enough attention to me," (criticism) try to say
   something like, "I felt really lonely this week." If you had a
   role to play in the problem, take personal responsibility for
   how you could improve. For example, you might say, "I was
   lonely this week, and I know that spending so much time
   on my laptop might have contributed to that." Lastly, ask
   your partner for their perception by saying something like,
   "How did you see the things I am talking about?" Work to
   be open to their perception.

4. **Discuss agenda items.** Come prepared to discuss topics
   that need problem-solving, consensus, or change. Some
   couples write topics on a whiteboard over the week so they
   don't forget them; others keep a Google Doc. And if you're
   like me, you might just jot it on a piece of paper right before
   you're going to chat. Topics you might keep track of include
   concerns you've had over the week, decisions you need to
   make, a story you've wanted to share, or an argument you
   want to revisit.

5. **Pick at least one or two of the agenda items to explore
   together.** Make an agreement to come up with temporary
   solutions to the issues together.

Your first weekly meeting is going to look a little bit different than
the others. During your first meeting, I want you to do steps 1 through
3 and then explore:

- Your inventory
- Your baskets

YOUR INVENTORY

After step 3 of the meeting, sit down together and explore an inventory of your lives. This is a list of your thirds.

Here are some areas you'll want to take a cursory glance at:

- What is using your time?

- What is using your money?

- What is requiring your emotional and psychological focus?

- What is impacting your health?

In this inventory, include everything—the positive, neutral, and negative weights within your life. Try to get as granular as you can. The smaller things are often where you will start to make changes because they are easier to fix, and having the opportunity to identify these fixes can help you get some early wins.

For example, when taking inventory of your finances, you might initially include only the things that are really stressing you out—like the mortgage on your house or the car loan that is too high. I want to encourage you to also include smaller expenses, like the subscriptions you are signed up for.

Don't let perfect be the enemy of good here. Just create a list based on what you know. You can do more investigating over time, but try not to let yourself get stuck on creating this inventory.

Once you've got your combined list, you are going to think about which of the items go into basket 1, shedding.

BASKETS

Now we are going to take the items on your inventory and move them into baskets to help you start to manage the stress in your life. Use three pieces of paper. Label the first page "Basket 1: Shedding," the second page "Basket 2: Preventing," and the final page "Basket 3: Adapting." Once you do that you are ready to move to the next section.

BASKET 1: SHEDDING

When a couple's lives feel unmanageable, they should first look at what they need to shed. How can they get rid of the layers that make life daunting and heavy?

While most people recognize that shedding will result in feeling lighter and clearer, there tends to be a lot of resistance in this area when it comes to making decisions and taking action. Whether I am talking to parents who need to stop focusing on dirty shoes on the floor or a couple who needs to give the home renovations a break for a little bit, most people don't *want* to actually offload anything.

Keyword: *want*.

We've become a very want-driven society, and because of this our needs often get kicked to the curb. I know you *want* to do all of your hobbies. I know you *want* to be able to take your children to Disney World. I know you *want* to take on another job responsibility. But can you? Is it getting you what you need?

Worse than wanting, though, is that you've likely been told you *should* be able to have it or *should* be able to make the time to do it.

So, when I present this offload box to a couple, they've already been programmed to resist me. "Who are you to tell me what I can have and what I want?" or "What failing must live within us that we can't make it all work?"

We need to step away from the entitlement that we can have everything and the pressure that we should be able to.

You just can't. You need to prioritize.

Shedding is going to be your largest basket. It will include all of the things in your life that you can shed. These are the things that are most in your control, even if it seems daunting to control them. As you and your partner decide what to put into basket 1, I want you to remember that this is *temporary*. If you decide to start cutting the grass on your own to save some money, it doesn't mean you have to do it forever. If you decide to put a pause on taking classes, it doesn't mean you can't take a class later.

All of the work you are doing now is uncomfortable, but it is the act of making small sacrifices to simplify your life and take control so you can enjoy your relationship together. For your shedding box, follow these steps:

Step 1: Go through your list together and circle everything that you can easily let go of. For example, you might not have an emotional attachment to your Netflix account. Perhaps you've wanted to cancel it for a while but haven't had the time.

Step 2: After your first look through the list you should have circled some things that feel simple to let go of. I want you to go through the list again and push yourself to let go of more.

When thinking of what to let go of, ask yourself:

- Is this stressor something that I am unable to remove from my life? There are some stressors in our lives that just exist in the moment and we can't remove them. We will talk more about what to do about those next. Those stressors won't stay in basket 1. Put a star next to these things so you can manage them later.

- Is this stressor something that aligns with our North Star? Remember, your North Star is the lifestyle and meaning that you and your partner are working on together. It is your big-picture goal. It has to do with your values. Go through your list again. If they go against your North Star goals, circle them.

You should have most of your list circled at this point. Move these items to basket 1. Continue on to basket 2, preventing.

BASKET 2: PREVENTING

There are certain stressors in life that we can't shed. Perhaps it's because they are integral to how we want to live or maybe it's because it's an obligation or commitment we are part of. Perhaps it's just that life happens and things happen and there is nothing you can do about it.

This is where basket 2, preventing, comes into play.

When you look at the things in your life that cause you stress, I want you to consider which items could become less stressful if you did the following:

- Came up with new systems

- Had better boundaries

- Got some help

- Took better care of yourself

- Co-regulated with your partner

Move these items to basket two.

New Systems

As your life gets into order, you'll have the opportunity to create new systems that will help you maintain the order. I often recommend that couples utilize Eve Rodsky's Fair Play card deck. Inside the deck are several different categories that relate to managing your home. Go through the cards together. As you look at each card, decide on who you think has current ownership of the task. The card might say something like, "Making doctor's appointments." Together you will decide who takes start-to-finish responsibility for the task.

By making it clear who owns a task, you can reduce the mental load it takes to remember it and increase feelings of fairness within the home. Your relationship will shift from a place of exhaustion and suffering when you come up with realistic systems that are clear.

Once couples know who has ownership, it makes their "job description" within the family much clearer. It doesn't mean they don't sometimes get help for the role they own, but it does mean they are responsible for researching, delegating, and getting the task completed.

The tasks don't need to be equal. They need to feel fair.

Boundaries

Some of the stressors in our lives can be prevented if we work on having better boundaries. As couples look at their basket 2 list together, I ask them to talk candidly with one another about which of the stressors are exacerbated by the fact that they don't have great boundaries around the issue. Boundaries can be the way we talk about issues or the limits we set around things like time, energy, and finances. Boundaries prevent overwhelm.

Getting Help

As you look over your basket 2 list, you might notice that some of the stress in your life could be significantly reduced by getting help. Getting help can be hard for many different reasons—you might struggle to find it because it is too expensive or maybe because the people around you are just as burdened as you are.

If you have financial means, you might get help by hiring a babysitter, getting a cleaning service, or paying someone to check your email. But those types of help are mostly available to those with financial means. Often, getting help is about building a community of friends, neighbors, and family who are willing to jump in when needed.

Help also doesn't have to be task-based; it can be emotional as well. Hugs, meaningful conversation, and spending time with people can be helpful ways to reduce stress.

Regardless, you need to build a level of comfort with recognizing when you need help and asking for it.

Getting help can bring a lot of relief to your life by reducing the tasks you need to perform. A word of caution, though, make sure that getting help isn't maintaining or adding to your stress. Sometimes, people get extra help when really they should find a way to negate the issue altogether. And sometimes, getting help is a sign that you've got so much going on in your life that you can't do the basics.

Go through your list thinking of your own needs, and see if there is any stress that could be reduced by asking for help.

Taking Care of Yourself

Make sure that you are allowing your stress cycle to complete. This means resting, eating, breathing, and moving your body. Doing these things will help you prevent levels of stress that result in burnout.

Co-Regulation

As you look at your basket 2 list, you might find that some of the issues wouldn't feel so awful if you could just learn to co-regulate in response to them. When people co-regulate, tense topics are less likely to escalate. This means that while something might not be ideal, you're still able to maintain a level head and stay connected while solving the issue.

When couples co-regulate, they can communicate more clearly, show affection, problem solve, set goals, and manage their anger so it doesn't become harmful.

Continue to basket 3, adapting.

BASKET 3: ADAPTING

Some stressors will exist regardless of the work we do to shed and prevent. People get sick. Jobs get busy. Exciting and big events have to be planned. The economy crashes. No one will live a stress-free life. In fact, you don't want to. Basket 3 is about looking at the stress in your life that exists either because it has to or because it's out of your control. Accepting doesn't mean liking. It does mean learning to adapt.

Adapting requires the following:

- Accepting reality

- Being responsible

- Utilizing coping skills

Move to basket three any items you need to adapt.

Accepting Reality

Accepting reality doesn't mean condoning the experience. It just means you look it straight in the eye and name it for what it is. Doing this will allow you and your partner to support each other and solve the problem.

Being Responsible

Needing to take responsibility for a difficult reality doesn't mean you haven't been responsible in other ways. It does mean that once you recognize the cards you've been dealt, you'll have to find a way to play them. This will allow you and your partner to make the choice to sit with the issue and find some peace, work toward change, or quit.

Using Coping Skills

If there is a stressor on your list that cannot be changed, you'll need to lean into your coping skills. All coping skills should have the goal of completing the stress cycle instead of continuing it. Sometimes, we use coping skills that continue the cycle, like drinking or adding more to our plates.

Instead, you want to work on breathing, spending time with people you love, and moving your body.

BACK TO SHEDDING

Now that you've thought through what needs to be prevented and what needs to be adapted, it's important to come back to your shedding basket. This basket holds everything that needs to go in the real or metaphorical garbage in order to improve your relationship.

For the issues that are low in importance, pick a weekly date where you will tackle them together. For example, you might need to clean out your closets in order to have a more organized house. Commit to taking an hour each Sunday to go through part of a closet. During this hour, do as much as you can—list things on neighborhood giveaway groups, drive to your local thrift shop to drop things off, and fold and organize the clothes you're going to keep.

For the issues that are more complicated, rate them in order of how challenging they feel. Maybe it feels most challenging to leave a job, but not as challenging to change your hours at the job. Negotiate together when shedding these more complex issues, remembering that your North Star—likely your family and well-being—are always more important than whatever issue is causing you and your relationship harm.

Everything Has Changed in a World That Is Still the Same

'm eight months pregnant with my second child, and I just dumped a laundry basket of clothes onto the floor of the baby's room. It's pouring outside and the room is dark and the air is heavy. It is July, and I haven't taken the time to put the air conditioner back on.

I just got a message from our contractor with a quote for the cost to remodel our garage into a playroom. A few weeks ago, I began feeling particularly anxious about space, and after being influenced by social media, decided we absolutely needed to add more room to our home.

"It'll be $30,000 to complete the project. We can get started whenever you want," the message said.

But today, I've had enough of a pause between the emotional need and thinking it through to decide that we absolutely don't need to add room to our home. *We have enough. It will be enough*, I remind myself.

"Thanks so much! That is a great quote. However, I've decided it's not an expense we should take on right now," I respond.

In the past, this message would have been excruciating to send—giving up something that I desired while also potentially disappointing this man who so willingly took the time to create a quote. But, I knew that if I took on this project and expense, my life would feel worse, not better.

I hop into my email and see at least three requests. I notice my heart rate starts to increase. *You're feeling anxious about this. It's a sign it's too much*, I think. And it is. I am about to have a baby and made the decision to do less, not more. And while I hate to disappoint and while I love to prove I can do it all, I've made a promise to myself not to lean into those impulses.

"I'd love to come on your podcast," I type. "Thank you so much for thinking of me. Right now I'm not able to schedule anything, but let me know if you need names of some people who can!" Phew. Boundaries. They feel better every day.

I've recently left a position that was really important to me but wasn't allowing me the freedom I needed to be with my family and to live out my values the way I'd like. The loss of the position meant the loss of half my salary. And yet, I feel at peace. It's going to take giving up a lot of things that now cost too much, but that's okay.

I look up at the clock and notice it's 4:10 pm. Shit, I forgot to take my son to karate. I've been here writing this book. But that's okay. My husband's got it because he shares the mental load with me. I didn't really need to remember.

Over the past six years, I have been on the same journey that so many of the couples in this book have been on—trying to figure out how to take on less, be responsible for my own lifestyle, and adapt and accept what cannot be changed. I've worked with my partner to create a more sustainable lifestyle, one where we've both learned to practice better boundaries, allocate the family workload more fairly, and take care of ourselves individually.

And while absolutely nothing I do will protect me from all stress—we experienced multiple deaths this year, I've had employees that I care about get really sick, I had a miscarriage and difficult birth, and we've faced unexpected and upsetting expenses—the lives we've created insulate us from it becoming excruciating stress that ruins our relationship. We are no longer bringing constant stress onto ourselves and recognize that there are better ways to regulate, connect, and problem solve.

When I come home at the end of the day and feel my husband is distant, I don't get angry with him. I work with him to explore what's going on and to figure out if stress is beneath the mood. When I am struggling, he doesn't fight me or try to problem solve. He helps me to process what's going on and allows me to work on reducing my stress before anything else.

I've started leaning out of opportunities big and small. I don't need to do more. I am okay with things being just enough. It's the year of no.

And this has given me so much opportunity to truly lean into the things that matter and say yes to the most important relationships I have.

All couples argue, but if you can't seem to improve your relationship, it's likely that stress is underlying it all. Tackling stress in our relationships requires us to first recognize that stress is a physiological process, then to learn how to self-regulate and co-regulate, and finally, to commit to a system of shedding, preventing, and adapting to the stress within our lives.

When we tackle stress, we tackle our relationship ills, and in doing so we create more space for partnership. We become more able to be patient, kind, and caring. We open up to humor, play, and curiosity. And, we are able to dream and build, together.

Acknowledgments

This book is possible because of my community, a community that helps me navigate the stress of writing a book, running a business, and raising kids. Thank you first and foremost to my husband, Andrew, who gave me the time I needed to write and edit this book. The way he talked me through my stress and anxieties in regard to the content of this book is an example of how he supports and believes in me. Thank you to Laura Lee Mattingly, my wonderful agent and friend, who took the time to read my proposal, believe in it, and send it along to Sounds True. Thank you to Diana Ventimiglia, my second-time editor extraordinaire, who is warm and positive and full of ideas. It's scary being vulnerable, and someone like Diana makes it easier—she's a great co-regulator! To my friends, who cheer me on, and my work wife, Ariel Stern, who helps me flesh out my ideas regarding relationships. Thank you to Don Cole, who worked closely with Ariel and me as we were developing our skills and helped us more fully understand the concept of emotional flooding and stress. And to all the teachers and colleagues who inspired me with the wonderful work they do.

Notes

CHAPTER 1

1. Liz Dean, Brendan Churchhill, and Leah Ruppanner, "The Mental Load: Building a Deeper Theoretical Understanding of How Cognitive and Emotional Labor Overload Women and Mothers," *Community, Work & Family* 25, no. 1 (November 2021): 13–29, doi.org/10.1080/13668803.2021.2002813.
2. John M. Gottman, Carrie Cole, and Donald L. Cole, "Four Horsemen in Couple and Family Therapy," *Encyclopedia of Couple and Family Therapy* (October 2019): 1212–16, doi.org/10.1007/978-3-319-49425-8_179.
3. John M. Gottman, *What Predicts Divorce?* (Psychology Press, 1993).

CHAPTER 2

1. Lisa Feldman Barrett, *Seven and a Half Lessons About the Brain* (Houghton Mifflin Harcourt, 2020).
2. Zara Abrams, "High Stress Levels During the Pandemic Are Making Even Everyday Choices Difficult to Navigate," *American Psychological Association: Monitor on Psychology* (June 1, 2022): apa.org/monitor/2022/06/news-pandemic-stress-decision-making.
3. Adela C. Timmons, Reout Arbel, and Gayla Margolin, "Daily Patterns of Stress and Conflict in Couples: Associations with Marital Aggression and Family-of-Origin Aggression," *Journal of Family Psychology* 35, no. 1 (February 2017): 93–104, doi.org/10.1037/fam0000227.

4. Ashley K. Randall and Guy Bodenmann, "The Role of Stress on Close Relationships and Marital Satisfaction," *Clinical Psychology Review* 29, no. 2 (March 2009): 105–15, doi.org/10.1016/j.cpr.2008.10.004.

CHAPTER 3

1. Office of Planning, Research & Evaluation, Administration for Children & Families, "Self-Regulation Training Approaches and Resources to Improve Staff Capacity for Implementing Healthy Marriage Programs for Youth," US Department of Health & Human Services, accessed April 14, 2023, acf.hhs.gov/opre/project/self-regulation-training-approaches-and-resources-improve-staff-capacity-implementing.
2. Todd F. Heatherton and Dylan D. Wagner, "Cognitive Neuroscience of Self-Regulation Failure," *Trends in Cognitive Sciences* 15, no. 3 (March 2011): 132–39, doi.org/10.1016/j.tics.2010.12.005.

CHAPTER 4

1. Emily Nagoski, *Come As You Are* (Simon & Schuster, 2015).
2. Guy Bodenmann et al., "The Association Between Daily Stress and Sexual Activity," *Journal of Family Psychology* 24, no. 3 (June 2010): 271–79, doi.org/10.1037/a0019365; Lisa Dawan Hamilton and Cindy M. Meston, "Chronic Stress and Sexual Function in Women," *Journal of Sexual Medicine* 10, no. 10 (October 2013): 2443–54, doi.org/10.1111/jsm.12249; Ludek Fiala, Jiri Lenz, and Rachel Sajdlova, "Effect of Increased Prolactin and Psychosocial Stress on Erectile Function," *Andrologia* 53, no. 4 (May 2021): doi/10.1111/and.14009.
3. H. Lejeune, É. Huyghe, and S. Droupy, "Diminution du désir sexuel et déficit en testostérone chez l'homme [Hypoactive Sexual Desire and Testosterone Deficiency in Men]," *Progres en Urologie* 23, no. 9 (July 2013): 621–28, doi.org/10.1016/j.purol.2013.01.019; Anneliese Schwenkhagen and John Studd, "Role of Testosterone in the Treatment of Hypoactive Sexual Desire Disorder," *Maturitas* 63, no. 2 (June 2009): 152–59, doi.org/10.1016/j.maturitas.2009.02.011.

CHAPTER 5

1. Beth Berry, *Motherwhelmed: Challenging Norms, Untangling Truths, and Restoring Our Worth to the World* (Revolution from Home, 2020).

CHAPTER 6

1. "Cope," Vocabulary.com Dictionary, accessed November 27, 2023, vocabulary.com/dictionary/cope.
2. Esther Perel and Mary Alice Miller, "Rituals for Healthy Relationships at Every Stage," EstherPerel.com, estherperel.com/blog/rituals-for-healthy-relationships.
3. William J. Doherty, *The Intentional Family: How to Build Family Ties in Our Modern World* (Da Capo Livelong Books, 1997).

CHAPTER 7

1. Stan Tatkin, "Wired for Love: The Couple Bubble," The Art of Living Retreat Center, artoflivingretreatcenter.org/blog/wired-for-love-the-couple-bubble.
2. Joanna Syrda, "Spousal Relative Income and Male Psychological Distress," *Personality and Social Psychology Bulletin* 46, no. 6 (June 2020): 976–92, doi.org/10.1177/0146167219883611.

CHAPTER 8

1. Weight Watchers, "Oprah's 2020 Vision Tour Visionaries: Lady Gaga Interview," YouTube, retrieved November 27, 2023, youtube.com/watch?v=f8iNYY7YVO4.
2. Haruki Murakami, *What I Talk About When I Talk About Running: A Memoir* (Anchor Canada, 2013).
3. Marsha M. Linehan, *DBT Skills Training Handouts and Worksheets*, 2nd ed. (Guilford Press, 2014).
4. Luc Rochette, Geoffrey Dogon, and Catherine Vergely, "Stress: Eight Decades After Its Definition by Hans Selye: 'Stress Is the Spice of Life,'" *Brain Sciences* 13, no. 2 (2023): 310, doi.org/10.3390/brainsci13020310.

CHAPTER 9

1. Uri Weinblatt and Haim Omer, "Nonviolent Resistance: A Treatment for Parents of Children with Acute Behavior Problems," *Journal of Marital and Family Therapy* 31, no. 1 (January 2008): 75–92, doi.org/10.1111/j.1752-0606.2008.00054.x; "NVR Principles," NVR Action & Practice CIC (2017), nvrtraining.org/nvr-principles.

About the Author

Elizabeth Earnshaw, LMFT, CGT, is a couples therapist and the author of *I Want This To Work*. She is the founder and director of A Better Life Therapy, a national practice that helps people improve their relationships.

Elizabeth lives in West Chester, Pennsylvania, with her husband, son, daughter, and labradoodle.

About Sounds True

Sounds True was founded in 1985 by Tami Simon with a clear mission: to disseminate spiritual wisdom. Since starting out as a project with one woman and her tape recorder, we have grown into a multimedia publishing company with a catalog of more than 3,000 titles by some of the leading teachers and visionaries of our time, and an ever-expanding family of beloved customers from across the world.

In more than three decades of evolution, Sounds True has maintained our focus on our overriding purpose and mission: to wake up the world. We offer books, audio programs, online learning experiences, and in-person events to support your personal growth and awakening, and to unlock our greatest human capacities to love and serve.

At SoundsTrue.com you'll find a wealth of resources to enrich your journey, including our weekly *Insights at the Edge* podcast, free downloads, and information about our nonprofit Sounds True Foundation, where we strive to remove financial barriers to the materials we publish through scholarships and donations worldwide.

To learn more, please visit SoundsTrue.com/freegifts or call us toll-free at 800.333.9185.

Together, we can wake up the world.

sounds true

WAKING UP THE WORLD